DR. DON BIERLE

with Linda Hanner

Emerald Books

P.O. Box 635
Lynnwood, Washington 98046

Table of Contents

Unit One - Searching for Real Life

Unit Two - Searching for a Reliable Record

Unit Three - Searching for the Real Jesus

Unit Four - Searching for a Reasonable Faith

Unit Five - Discovering Real Faith

Unit Six - Finding Real Life in Jesus

Notes

Introduction

How can we know if anyone is home in the universe?

Why does it matter?

Gail Maeder is dead. She committed suicide. Her motive?—A search for significance and hope in her life. She was one of the 39 members of the Heaven's Gate cult who gambled their lives on a passing comet. Here is what Gail wrote to her parents about two and one-half years earlier.

> Mom and Dad,
>
> You are probably wondering exactly what I've decided to do with my life. Until recently nothing had ever been able to offer me any real motivation. I wanted and needed more. This is why I couldn't play the regular games of this society. I felt like I had outgrown it, and I just really didn't see the point of it all.
>
> Love, Gail

A noble and valuable pursuit indeed, this seeking after purpose and meaning. We all want it. But how do we know we're looking for it in the right places? How do we know that the paths we take will not lead to despair and destruction? Does God know? How do we even know there *is* a God? Do we check our brains at the door of religion and just say we have faith? What is faith anyway?

The search for faith—that's what this book, FaithSearch, is about. Want some answers that make sense? Answers that will lead you to a life full of joy and purpose rather than despair and hopelessness?

Even though you might be coming from a different perspective—different than that of your peers, your teacher, or me—we can still team up to explore this issue of faith. Where do you stand? Can you relate to any of the following ideas and attitudes?

Where do you stand?

AMY is a senior in high school. She says she considers herself a Christian because her family attends a Christian church. She believes that Jesus was a messenger and the Son of God. But she is not sure that he *is* God. In recent years, she has been exposed to a spiritual philosophy that claims to include all religions. She kind of likes that idea. Christianity seems too narrow, too judgmental.

JIM is a college sophomore. Throughout high school he excelled academically and was star of the football team. Parents and teachers have assured him that he is really going to "go places." Yet, he admits to feeling pretty insecure about the future, about life in general. He has never attended church and doesn't see any need for that. He believes that religions were established to control people morally. He dismisses them as useful for some, but not for him. He scoffs at people who claim that their faith is real. Yet, sometimes he wishes he was "naive" enough to believe in something beyond this life.

ANDREA is a junior in high school. She became a committed Christian at a summer Bible camp when she was in seventh grade. Since then she has hung onto her faith. But it's hard. She's bombarded with messages that contradict what she reads in the Bible. She listens to her peers talk about going to parties, getting drunk, having sex. It bothers her that most of them don't seem interested in God. She wants to talk to them about him, but fears they'll be turned off—or that they'll ask questions she won't know how to answer.

TYLER is 17 and cynical about life. He dropped out of school this year. He works during the week just to support his weekend habit of partying, drinking and "getting high." For a time, he wondered about the meaning of life and the existence of God. He concluded there isn't any way to know for sure about those things. So it's no use trying to figure it out. Drugs and alcohol make it easier. At least, they make him feel good for awhile.

If you're finding it hard to know what to believe, it's not surprising. Some religions teach that you were created by God and can know him in a personal way. Others teach that God exists, but that he is like the "Force" of *Star Wars*—vague and impersonal. Science heavily promotes the view that all life—yours included—evolved from a single cell that was spontaneously generated by chance chemical reactions. Humanism teaches that you came into the world with no inherent worth and there are no absolute truths for you to live by. "New age" philosophers tell you that you are your own god and can control your own destiny. Whew!

Amidst such confusion, you are pressured to plan for your future—get an education, become successful. But media messages bombard you to "live for the moment"—to indulge in risky behaviors that provide temporary pleasure. Some of your peers pressure you to "just try it" regarding alcohol and mind-altering drugs.

So we're all different. We face temptations. We fail at times. But where you are as you begin this faith search isn't the most important thing. Most important is whether you're willing to be open—to care, to know, to change. Jesus Christ says it this way: *"Ask, and it shall be given to you; seek, and you shall find; knock, and it shall be opened to you. For everyone who asks receives, and he who seeks finds, and to him who knocks it shall be opened."* Matthew 7:7-8

Does Jesus really mean what he says? If we are willing to know what is really true, will we truly find meaning and happiness in life? In FaithSearch, I'd like to invite you to retrace the steps I traveled in my own search for significance and faith. My hope is that the discoveries I made will help you in your own faith search. We'll be asking questions like these:

- What is the purpose for my life?

- How can I know there is a God?

- Are all religions the same?

- Is the Bible historically true? Can I trust it for my life?

- Can faith be supported with facts?

- Is Jesus really God appearing on earth?

- What about doubts? Do they indicate I'm not a Christian?

- How can I know God personally?

Searching for Real Life

Is There Real Purpose?

unit one - day one

If you find the lyrics to the Beatle's "Nowhere Man" ringing true for you, but wishing they didn't, you have lots of company. John Lennon wrote the words over thirty years ago, yet they express the same theme that continues to dominate today's music—the seemingly futile search for significance.

> *"He's a real nowhere man*
> *sitting in his nowhere land*
> *making all his nowhere plans for nobody.*
> *Doesn't have a point of view,*
> *knows not where he's going to.*
> *Isn't he a bit like me and you?"*
>
> —lyrics from a song by John Lennon of the Beatles

These lyrics reveal that life is especially confusing when one's purpose is unclear. It's not as simple as playing sports, being part of a drama or working a job. In these cases the expectations are pretty clear—make a tackle, score a goal, recite lines, paint a picture, flip burgers, sell an item of clothing. The purpose of life itself is much more evasive.

Even those who seem to "have it all" often admit to feeling empty. The singer Madonna and the well-known actor Richard Dreyfuss are among those who have admitted to being unhappy in spite of achieving fame and fortune. During television interviews, Richard admitted that he envies those who have found inner peace, and Madonna revealed that fear is her almost constant companion.

People who don't understand how their lives can have ultimate meaning or purpose often desperately grasp for it in destructive ways. In an attempt to find happiness they indulge even more in the "things" of this world. Some become tragically addicted to drugs or alcohol.

On the other hand, some claim to have found peace and contentment through religious faith. But what is faith? Is it just an illusion—another form of "escapism"? Or is it reasonable—consistent with the facts in the real world?

FOR MEMORY

And without faith it is impossible to please God, because anyone who comes to him must believe that he exists and that he rewards those who earnestly seek him.

Hebrews 11:6

> *"...Seems like I should*
> *be getting somewhere.*
> *Somehow I'm neither*
> *here nor there*
> *Can you help me remember*
> *how to smile.*
> *Make it somehow*
> *all seem worthwhile."*
>
> —lyrics from "Runaway Train" by Soul Asylum

> *"Tired of lying in the sunshine*
> *staying home to watch the rain.*
> *You are young and life is long*
> *and there is time to kill today*
> *And then one day you find*
> *ten years have got behind you*
> *No one told you to run, you missed*
> *the starting gun."*
>
> —lyrics from "Time" by Pink Floyd

> **Blessed are those who hunger and thirst for righteousness for they will be filled.**
>
> **Matthew 5:6**

In a few sentences, explain your current perception of faith. At the end of this study, we'll invite you to do this again to see if and how your perception has changed.

_____

_____

_____

_____

_____

_____

A DOG'S LIFE

People have a need—an innate, inborn need to have a reason for their **doing** and even more for their **being**. We differ from animals in that we seem to have a built-in desire for something deeper than what our visible world offers. I doubt that your pet dog spends one moment a day questioning why he exists or pondering his future. As long as he has a daily dish of dog chow, a stick to chase, a soft rug and an occasional loving stroke from you, he is likely to be quite content.

There was a time when I was confused about faith. I saw it as kind of a crutch for weak, uneducated people. During my early college days, my "jock" friends and I mocked the religious types on campus.

Later as a biology graduate student, I couldn't wait for a certain religious magazine to arrive in another student's office. My colleagues and I would gather to make fun of the "naive" people who wrote it.

But as I was mocking, I was struggling inside. I wondered about death. I struggled with guilt, but didn't know why. I felt empty. I was searching for something to fill the void—and had been for several years. At first, I thought my athletic and academic performance would give me status and personal satisfaction. Later I looked to science for answers and significance. Little did I know then that a logical, "scientific" study would eventually lead me to the end of my search—a personal faith relationship with the infinite and creator God.

– Dr. Don

THINK ABOUT IT

Think about some of the ways that you pursue a sense of fulfillment or purpose. Rank each of the following choices according to the degree you think you do find or could find purpose from them (with 5 being the most likely to help provide purpose and 1 being the least likely to provide purpose).

Circle the ranking that fits best

	Least				Most
Being a good friend	1	2	3	4	5
Owning a car	1	2	3	4	5
Being a great student	1	2	3	4	5
Being good in sports	1	2	3	4	5
Being accepted by a prestigious college	1	2	3	4	5
Owning great stuff (stereo, clothes, etc.)	1	2	3	4	5
Good health	1	2	3	4	5
Being popular	1	2	3	4	5
Having a well-paying job	1	2	3	4	5
Getting along with family	1	2	3	4	5
Being loved	1	2	3	4	5
Being in love	1	2	3	4	5
Other_____	1	2	3	4	5

Do you think any of the above provides sufficient reason that you exist? Why or why not?

_____

_____

_____

What Is Real?

unit one - day two

Imagine with me that nothing exists—not planets or people. In place of what we know as the earth and universe is just an empty void. Then suddenly, out of the vacuum a large, spherical ball of soil appears!

I'll bet you couldn't name a purpose for the soil without assuming the existence of something else. You can't list purposes like growing plants or trees, or as a foundation for buildings because plants, trees and buildings don't yet exist. As long as they don't, there is nothing to give the soil purpose.

But what if some grass suddenly appears on the dirt? The dirt now has a purpose—to provide nutrients and a place for the grass to grow. But why is the grass there—what is *its* purpose? In the real world, we'd say it is for food or beauty or to provide turf for a soccer game.

Yet, in our imaginary world, nothing else exists to eat it, view it or make use of it. To solve that problem, let's bring in a cow. The grass now exists to feed the cow.

Yet, we have a new dilemma. What is the cow's purpose? To fertilize the grass? To produce milk? To be used in TV commercials? But for what or whom?

We could go on and on—this scenario would never end. Perhaps our problem is that no intelligent (reasoning) beings are present who can understand purpose—or appreciate the beauty of nature. So let's say human beings show up who can appreciate the usefulness of the soil, the grass and the cow.

Now we have what might appear to be a complete universe. However, this poses an interesting problem. Just as the soil, grass and cow each needed a purpose, we must figure out what is an adequate purpose for humans.

Can you name some possible purposes for this large sphere of soil?

GOT MILK?

THE REAL UNIVERSE

The imaginary universe described in this section is actually the universe we live in. The soil represents all the "matter," the grass and cow all plant and animal life, and we are the humans. The fact that there is more of each thing (many cows), and even more kinds of finite things (like planets, trees, aardvarks and ducks) doesn't solve the crisis of purpose and meaning.

**Consider the ravens:
They do not sow or
reap, they have no
storeroom or barn;
yet God feeds them.
And how much
more valuable you
are than birds!**

Luke 12:24

Alone in the universe

Why are the humans here? If the sphere of soil and the grass turf with a cow and humans walking on it are floating through an otherwise empty space, the humans can only dig in the dirt, mow the grass and milk the cow—until death. As the Russian novelist, Tolstoy, asked, "What is life for? To die?" This has been the timeless question of humanity.

That's because everything that exists is finite. The finite cannot know how it came into existence, why it exists at all, and what will happen to it after death. The sphere of soil and everything on it are floating through space as cosmic orphans without a source or reason for their existence.

The "so what" problem

So, if we are alone in the universe, why are we here? We are faced with the "so what" problem:

- I go to school, so...
- I can get good grades, so...
- I can go to a good college, so...
- I can get a good job, so...
- I can make a lot of money, so...
- I can buy the right car and have a big house, so...
- I have a family and send my kids to a good school, so...
- They can go to a good college, so...
- They can get a good job and make a lot of money...
  So what!

The connection of actions in the "so what" scenario is logical. On the surface, the actions might even seem good enough to provide meaning to life. But it is deceptive. No matter what series of actions you insert in the above scenario, you'll eventually come to the point of exclaiming: **SO WHAT!**

Actions lead to results, not reasons

The basketball game

The "so what" scenario includes no ultimate, eternal context for the actions listed. If life really is nothing more than simply relating one behavior or action to another, the American novelist Ernest Hemingway was right when he said, "Life is just a dirty trick, a short journey from nothingness to nothingness."

The problem with trying to find fulfillment in what we do is that our actions don't provide meaning in themselves, they just lead to other actions.

Significance for our finite lives must come from something (or someone) outside of our actions. To get the idea, think about a basketball game. A player might get real pumped up about pulling out the victory with the final shot while a thousand fans anxiously watch. The outcome of a game, a championship and even a career could hinge on whether the ball goes in or bounces off the rim.

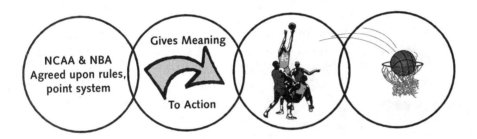

Points in a basketball game are assigned to a certain action. The action alone does not create its own significance. One could shoot hundreds of balls through the basket every day with no significance whatsoever. Neither can purpose and significance be found in the ball or the basket. The meaning of the ball going into the hoop exists because someone made up the game, assigned point values to baskets made and determined what those points would mean in the context of a game.

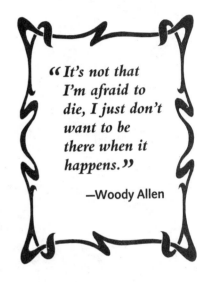

> "It's not that I'm afraid to die, I just don't want to be there when it happens."
>
> —Woody Allen

15

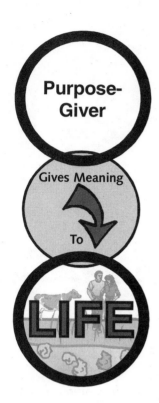

Purpose-Giver

Gives Meaning

To

LIFE

Language

Language provides another example of the need for something outside to provide significance to it.

Written language involves the use of symbols to convey meaning. Yet the symbols (letters) do not have significance in and of themselves. For example, take the symbols 'O', 'V', 'E' and 'L'. These symbols have no meaning by themselves. But grouped together in a certain order they can convey a powerful message. Why? Because meaning has been assigned them—in this case, a meaning that people have given them from the outside.

Meaning and significance to the "game of life"

All actions and events from womb to tomb can be as dramatic and exciting as a basketball game if we understand the rules in "playing the game" of life. Just as sports need designers who set up the game, life needs a designer or purpose-giver—something or someone who knows how we got here, why we're here and what difference our actions make to our destiny after death.

But how can we know that a purpose-giver is really there and not just the result of our wishful thinking or an overactive imagination? And if there is a real purpose-giver, how would we find out if it's "something" or "someone." Is there any way to know?

THINK ABOUT IT

Describe a few more examples of the principle that meaning must come from something outside of actions themselves (e.g., earning money, attending school classes):

_____

_____

Can you think of any action in your life that provides significance in itself—that does not derive significance from or is not defined by something outside itself? I think you'll find it true that meaning (in all areas of life, including life itself) must come from actions or events outside of ourselves.

Straight ahead we'll continue our faith search. I think you're going to be surprised at our discoveries.
– Dr. Don

Are There Real Options?

unit one - day three

As we discussed in the last section, logical thinking brings us to the conclusion that if life is to be more than just an endless chain of actions and behaviors, a purpose-giver must exist. The fact that there has been a consistent belief in "god" throughout civilization shows that people intuitively understand the need for something outside of life to provide purpose and meaning (the need for conclusions, not simply connections). But how can we know what that "outside something" is?

How can we know that a god is really there and not just the result of our imaginations? Just believing in a god doesn't make that god real. There needs to be an **objective** way of knowing. The good news is that there *is* one! But before we explore that further, we need to determine whether the purpose-giver is "something" or "someone."

Two essential traits of the purpose-giver of life

Remember, a purpose-giver of life must be capable of providing ultimate meaning and significance to all the actions in our finite (limited) world. Otherwise it would simply add another link to the chain of dependency in our search for purpose.

What does the purpose-giver need to be like to provide meaning and purpose to life? Many characteristics would be useful, but there are two that are essential:

1. The purpose-giver must be INFINITE

Purpose and significance need to be **inherent** to a purpose-giver of life. That way nothing outside it will be required to give it meaning. An <u>infinite</u> purpose-giver will stop the endless chain of needing something else.

The purpose-giver must be able to:

DO EVERYTHING (be omnipotent)—have the power to make matter, plants, animals and humans out of nothing and make everything work in perfect relationship and precision.

THE CYCLE OF DEPENDENCY

Remember that our universe, represented by dirt, grass, a cow and people, was caught in an endless chain of dependency. Likewise, if purpose were not inherent in the purpose-giver's nature, we could rightly ask, "What is the purpose-giver's purpose?" And the quest for purpose would go on—and on.

DEFINITIONS

Objective: Something real and observable (buildings and actions are objective; ideas are subjective).

Infinite: Something that is complete and perfect; totally independent of any need.

Inherent: Being a natural and essential part of someone or something.

As a high school student and later as a science major in college, I often pondered how I could know if God was really there. Just believing he was there didn't make sense to me. After all, I reasoned, believing there is a purple elephant in my room doesn't put one there.
– Dr. Don

We never talk anymore. Most of us don't talk to vegetables, bicycles or tall buildings. We don't expect a mutual relationship with our pet goldfish, a fire hydrant or a tree. That's because these things aren't personal.

KNOW EVERYTHING (be omniscient)—know how the finite things came into existence, why they exist, and what will happen to it all in the future.

BE EVERYWHERE (be omnipresent)—have the capability of being present everywhere in the universe simultaneously in order to sustain the principles and laws that govern it.

We now have our first indication that the purpose-giver must be "someone," not "something." Things don't have IQs. Knowing everything requires intellect—and that's a mark of a personal being. This leads us directly to the second essential characteristic of a purpose-giver of life.

2. The purpose-giver must be PERSONAL

A personal being not only has intellect, but will and emotion as well. Only a personal being is truly free to make choices, verbally communicate and interact in relationships that involve emotions like love. A purpose-giver that is infinite, but not personal, could not communicate with us or love us. The "Force" of *Star Wars* is impersonal—a "something," not "someone." A relationship with the Force would be like trying to have a relationship with electricity or a cosmic ray. Only a purpose-giver that is personal could tell us clearly how we got here, why we are here, and what will happen to us when die.

A QUICK REVIEW

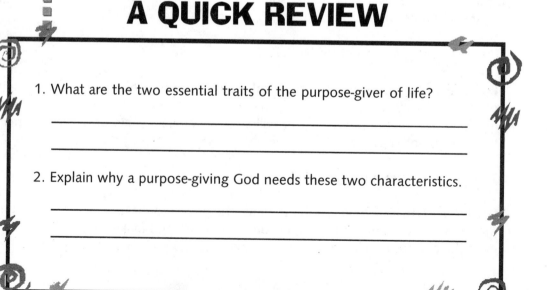

1. What are the two essential traits of the purpose-giver of life?

_____

_____

2. Explain why a purpose-giving God needs these two characteristics.

_____

_____

Gods, Gods, Everywhere

unit one - day four

We've established that the purpose-giver is "someone" not "something." And we know that this "someone" must be an infinite and personal being who is able to communicate our ultimate purpose and meaning to us.

Religions old and new all claim to have a purpose-giver they call "god" or "gods."

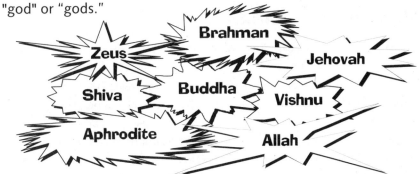

Are all these gods pretty much the same? Can they really provide purpose? Let's take a closer look at these gods of major world religions to see whether they possess the two essential traits of a purpose-giving god.

1. Eastern religions

Some examples of Eastern religions are Buddhism and Hinduism. Followers of these religions teach that "all is one" and "all is God." This means that the soil, grass, cows and even people are all part of God. Clearly they see God as INFINITE. But if *all* is God, that means all the evil around and in us is God, too. And a God that encompasses things like mud, cacti, and TV antennas can't be personal—have intelligence, will or emotion. In other words, Eastern religions teach there is really no one out there—no one to love or communicate, no "someone" that we can get to know. The gods of Eastern religions can't communicate life's ultimate purpose.

2. Western religions

The Greek and Nordic peoples developed a different idea. They wrote about gods that are very humanlike—very PERSONAL. But those of you who are familiar with Greek mythology know that these Greek gods and goddesses have more troubles than people do! They fight, lust and lie.

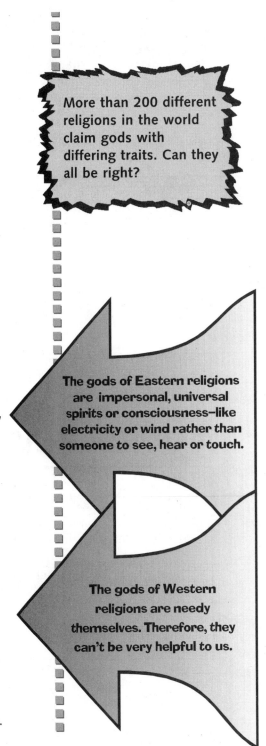

More than 200 different religions in the world claim gods with differing traits. Can they all be right?

The gods of Eastern religions are impersonal, universal spirits or consciousness—like electricity or wind rather than someone to see, hear or touch.

The gods of Western religions are needy themselves. Therefore, they can't be very helpful to us.

Their limitations and imperfections show that they are not infinite. Instead they are also part of the finite world, and have the same need as we do for an infinite purpose-giver.

3. Judaism, Islam and Christianity

A third type of world religion is represented by Judaism, Christianity and Islam. These religions all claim that God is both INFINITE and PERSONAL. They all teach that God is the complete and perfect creator of the world and the universe and that he can communicate purpose to us in a verbal and understandable way.

> Can any of the world religions provide a satisfactory answer to the question raised by atheist Anthony Flew: "Just how does what you call an invisible, intangible, eternally elusive gardener [god] differ from an imaginary gardener [god] or even no gardener [god] at all?"

AN ATHEIST'S PARABLE

Once upon a time two explorers came upon a clearing in the jungle. In the clearing were growing many flowers and many weeds. One explorer says, "Some gardener must tend this plot." The other disagrees, "There is no gardener." So they pitch their tents and set a watch. No gardener is ever seen. "But perhaps he is an invisible gardener." So They set up a barbed wire fence. They electrify it. They patrol with bloodhounds. But no shrieks ever suggest that some intruder has received a shock. No movements of the wire ever betray an invisible climber. The bloodhounds never give cry. Yet, still the believer is not convinced. "But there is a gardener—invisible, insensible to electric shocks, a gardener who comes secretly to look after the garden which he loves." At last the skeptic despairs, "But what remains of your original assertion? Just how does what you call an invisible, intangible, eternally elusive gardener differ from an imaginary gardener or even from no gardener at all?" [1]

—Anthony Flew

A QUICK REVIEW

Fill in the blanks:

Eastern religions teach that God is _____ but not _____.

Western religions teach that God is _____ but not _____.

Judaism, Christianity and Islam teach that God is both _____ and _____.

"Prove it"

Judaism, Islam and Christianity are alike in that they all claim a god that has the two traits essential for a purpose-giver to the finite world. But there is a significant point that distinguishes Christianity from the other two religions. It is revealed in the way that Christians answer the question: *How do I know that an infinite and personal God really exists?* Atheist Dr. Flew would say, "Prove it!" Just saying that you believe in God doesn't prove that one really exists.

The BIG question: "How can we know that God exists?"

Jews and Muslims would both say they know God exists because he revealed himself and talked to certain people— their prophets. The Jews base their beliefs on the Pentateuch, which contains what Moses claimed God told him. Muslims follow the Koran written by Muhammad based on messages he, too, says were given to him by God. Since Jews and Muslims both claim a God who communicates, they obviously believe that God is personal. In addition, Moses and Muhammad both say that their God claims he is the infinite creator of the universe. Yet certain parts of the messages of Judaism and Islam contradict each other. Is God confused and giving contradictory messages?

It's easy to feel uncertain if God is invisible, intangible and elusive. Was it really God who talked to Moses and Muhammad? Throughout history, almost every founder of a religious movement has claimed to have had a revelation from God. But in every case, that God is "out there somewhere" and cannot be seen or touched. In other words, he is invisible and intangible.

FOR MEMORY

"I am the way, the truth and the life."

Jesus in John 14:6 (NKJV)

CHRISTIANS CLAIM THAT THEIR GOD WALKED ON EARTH AND IS PART OF REAL HISTORY

Christianity alone claims that its founder was the infinite God. If the claim is true, it is only through a relationship with Jesus Christ that finite beings in a finite world can truly interact with the infinite to discover ultimate purpose.

DEFINITION

Pentateuch: The first five books of the Old Testament in the Bible

Incarnation: The term Christians use to describe God's coming to earth in the form and nature of man.

The BIG answer: God became flesh

Christianity is unique from all other religions in that Christians say they know that God exists because he did not remain invisible, intangible and elusive. According to them, he actually came to our earth as a human being and lived here for more than 33 years as the person of Jesus Christ.

Can Christians prove that God came to earth as Jesus Christ? Christianity, in fact, is the only religion that provides us an opportunity to investigate its God in history—to determine whether its claim is true. In upcoming chapters, our goal will be to do just that.

THINK ABOUT IT

Identify some concerns that come to mind when you consider that Jews and Muslims both claim to have gotten messages from the one true God, yet their messages contradict each other.

_____

_____

_____

_____

Why is the Christian claim that God became a human on earth so significant to our faith search?

_____

_____

_____

The "God Hypothesis"

unit one - day five

What does reason have to do with faith?

It's not out of line to want logical reasons for believing. After all, if God created us, he also gave us our reasoning, questioning minds. It doesn't make sense that he would expect us not to use our minds to ponder his existence and his nature. Wouldn't a caring God want to provide us with evidence of his existence and his personal concern?

As we proceed on our faith search, we'll explore opportunities to test the notion that the God of Christianity exists. We'll refer to the idea that God came to earth in the person of Jesus as the **"God hypothesis."**

Our review of world religions has shown that Christianity is unique in being the only religion that offers the opportunity in history to verify or discredit its claims about God. It is the only religion that says God made himself visible and tangible to the natural world—the world of reason and evidence.

Taking a scientific approach, our first challenge is to see if the "God hypothesis" is what scientists call a "testable hypothesis."

Is the "God hypothesis" testable?

There are three conditions required of a testable hypothesis:

1. It must be a "reasonable pursuit."
   (There must be a means to gather measurable evidence for the claim made.)

2. There must be a "method of proof."
   (There must be a way to evaluate data and weigh its validity.)

3. It must involve honesty.
   (Our attitude can't be, "Don't confuse me with facts, my mind is made up.")

Is it okay to question who God is?

Can God's existence be proven?

Before I became a believer, I often secretly wondered about people who said they simply "believed" without feeling a need for evidence on which to base their belief. These people would tell me, "Don, God is the answer."

But when I asked how they knew there was a God, they would respond that I must "just believe it." This would only reinforce my view that "religious" people were anti-intellectual. Reason, it seemed, had nothing to do with faith.

– Dr. Don

DEFINITION
Hypothesis: The scientific term for an idea or belief that has not yet been proven.

Does the "God hypothesis" meet the three conditions of a testable hypothesis? Let's check it out.

Is something that happened 2,000 years ago testable?

CONDITION #1
A reasonable pursuit: *A means of gathering evidence.*

According to Christians, the visit by God occurred nearly 2,000 years ago. Is it reasonable to conclude that Jesus Christ was God? It is reasonable if the New Testament writings, which tell about Jesus, are trustworthy eyewitness sources of information.

Fortunately there is an accepted method used by universities for judging ancient documents which we can apply to the New Testament. By studying the manuscript evidence and discoveries from the science of archaeology we can determine if the four gospels of the New Testament are reliable records. If they are, the first condition of the test will be satisfied since these documents will then qualify as sources of evidence concerning Jesus.

CONDITION #2
A method of proof: *A way to evaluate and weigh the data.*

When one sets out to prove something, there must be a way to evaluate the evidence and weigh its validity. There also must be some agreement about what constitutes proof of the hypothesis.

When it comes to testing something in the natural world, the scientific method can be used. In other words, the hypothesis can be tested through experiments done in a controlled setting where results can be observed.

But how do we test something that happened once—and long ago? Obviously, we can't repeat history in order to observe it. Therefore, our society accepts another method for proving past events—the legal method. It's the kind of test used by our system of courts, judges and juries. The evidence for two opposing sides of an issue are presented. A jury (or judge) then considers the evidence and makes a judgment about the issue.

As we move along on our faith search, we'll use the legal method to test the "God hypothesis." As jury members, we will weigh the evidence to decide for ourselves whether the "God hypothesis" is proven beyond a reasonable doubt.

THE GOSPELS
Matthew, Mark, Luke and John are the titles of the gospels that claim to be eyewitness accounts of Jesus' time on earth.

THE CASE ON TRIAL
Did the infinite and personal God of the universe come to earth as the God-man Jesus Christ?

CONDITION #3
Honesty with the evidence.

In looking at evidence for or against an issue, it's important to respond honestly. If you make up your mind beforehand, there's no point in reviewing the facts. An honest skeptic (unlike the dishonest skeptic in the story in the margin) bases his conclusion on the "facts" that are gathered and analyzed.

Called to "jury duty"

We're now ready to bring the case to court. Our first task will be to check out the evidence pertinent to the first condition: Are the four gospels reliable records of Jesus? We'll do that next. After that, we'll consider the evidence for the God hypothesis—members of the jury, we'll be asked to cast our votes.

This jury duty should be a fascinating experience. In fact, casting your personal vote regarding the evidence for Jesus is by far the most important vote that you'll ever be asked to make!

A DISHONEST SKEPTIC
A man announced to his family and coworkers that he was dead. When his wife took him to the local psychiatrist, he was told to research the medical journals until he had a firm conviction on the question: Do dead people bleed? After weeks of reading, he returned with the verdict. The evidence was overwhelming that dead people do not bleed. The psychiatrist smiled, grabbing a pin he'd set aside for this very moment. He poked the man's finger and waited for the man's response as blood dripped from his finger. The man turned pale and cried, "Amazing! Dead people do bleed after all!"

TEST YOUR MEMORY

Fill in the blanks:

1. The scientific method relies on studying evidence that is repeatable and can be _____ in a controlled environment.

2. The legal method relies on careful consideration of information about an issue by a _____ and _____.

3. List the three conditions of a testable hypothesis:

_____

_____

_____

unit two

Searching for a Reliable Record

Ancient Writings:
How to Know If They're Real

unit two - day one

Is the Bible we use today the same as that which was written nearly 2,000 years ago?

The Bible claims that the man Jesus Christ was also God. According to the writers of the New Testament, Jesus revealed that he was God by what he said and did. This is the Christian claim that we'll seek evidence to prove. As I mentioned earlier, I'm calling this the "God hypothesis."

As judge and jury, our first task in testing the God hypothesis is to examine the evidence. We'll start by looking at two questions:

> 1. **Are the writings of the New Testament of the Bible authentic? (Were they written by eyewitnesses who really knew Jesus?)**
>
> 2. **Do the New Testament writings have integrity? (Has the information that was written 2,000 years ago come down to us without significant change?)**

Literary scholars in every major university seek to answer the same questions. They have come up with methods to help us do so. These methods are called the principles of **historiography**. They are used for verifying information contained in classics (like those of Aristotle and Plato) and information about well-known historical people (such as Julius Caesar and Herodotus).

FOR MEMORY

Many have undertaken to draw up an account of the things that have been fulfilled among us, just as they were handed down to us by those who from the first were eyewitnesses and servants of the word.

Luke 1:1-2

EYEWITNESSES
The eyewitnesses who wrote most extensively about Jesus were Matthew, Mark, Luke and John. The books they wrote became the first four books of the New Testament.

DEFINITION
Historiography: The study of history. A historiographer is a history writer.

29

ACCURACY

Copies of ancient manuscripts have integrity only to the degree that they match the original.

CAESAR

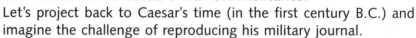

Caesar's War Commentaries was written about 50 B.C., more than 2,000 years ago. It is the personal memoirs of Julius Caesar's many brilliant military campaigns.

How accurate are ancient writings?

Before moving on, it might be helpful to explain how ancient literary writings were passed on to us. Have you ever wondered how our current knowledge of ancient history has been attained? Years ago, it wasn't so simple to reproduce copies of written documents. Take for instance the ancient book titled *Caesar's War Commentaries*. Let's project back to Caesar's time (in the first century B.C.) and imagine the challenge of reproducing his military journal.

Caesar has completed his writing. A friend visits his palace, sees the book and wants a copy for his own library. Caesar gives him permission to make one, but there are no photocopy machines in his office and no computer-stored files from which to print more copies. The friend must hire a trained copyist who works for days, handwriting every letter, word and sentence of Caesar's journal. Would this new copy be exactly like Caesar's original? That's unlikely.

Now suppose someone else sees the copy owned by Caesar's friend and gets permission to make a hand copy from it. Will this new copy be exactly like the first copy? That is also unlikely. In fact, it is probably less like Caesar's original than the first copy. Copies have integrity only to the degree that they match the original. Any changes on these first few copies are probably minor, but when you multiply the scenario by hundreds of copies over centuries of time, the changes accumulate. The accuracy is certain to deteriorate.

WHAT DO YOU KNOW?

Fill in the blanks based on the information above:

1. We know that a writing is authentic if it is written by

_____.

2. We know that a writing has integrity if it has been passed on over time without

_____.

3. Literary scholars use methods called _____

_____ to determine if ancient writings are authentic.

Not until the invention of the printing press (1,500 years later) was it possible to make exact copies of Caesar's journal. But how good were the handwritten copies that finally made it to the first printing presses? How much of Caesar's original writing remains today? The best way to know is to compare today's copy with his autograph (his handwritten original). But I can't do that because the original has never been found. In fact, no original copy of any ancient document has ever been found. Therefore, the integrity of ancient documents can be determined only by comparing the available copies with each other.

DEFINITION
Autograph: A handwritten original of an ancient document.

You might enjoy history or dread having to study it. In either case, I suspect that you pretty much accept the information you read about in your history books as fact. I know I once did. But I was surprised at what my research revealed.

– Dr. Don

A QUICK REVIEW

Check your memory with this brief true/false quiz (circle the correct choice):

1. An autograph is an original copy of an ancient work.   True   False

2. We have original copies of most ancient works.   True   False

3. To have integrity, a copy must closely match the original work.   True   False

The New Testament:
Putting It to the Real Test

unit two - day two

A three-part test will determine the accuracy of the Bible.

There is a test used by scholars to determine the accuracy of writings that have been copied for centuries. It is based on three major questions:

1. How many manuscripts (handwritten copies) have been found?

2. How early were the manuscripts written?

3. How accurately were the manuscripts copied?

We want to determine if the New Testament written in English today is an accurate copy of the version written in the Greek language of the first century. We'll put it to the three-part test.

1. How many handwritten New Testament copies have been found?

The more copies of a particular ancient manuscript found the better. A large number of copies allows scholars to compare them to find inconsistencies and to restore the most likely original wording. Also, the more copies, the easier it is to detect and correct any later intentional changes.

When I first learned that the New Testament far surpassed all other ancient documents in number of handwritten copies, I was a skeptic. I still didn't think the New Testament could be trusted. I imagined that there were good intellectual reasons to back me up. But I had never even questioned the accuracy of other ancient works that I read. I realize now that my problem was ignorance of the facts.

– Dr. Don

TONS OF COPIES!

Handwritten copies of most ancient writings are rare, but over 14,500 handwritten copies of the New Testament have been found![1]

When you take into account lectionaries that contain portions of the New Testament used for reading in ancient church services, there are over 24,000 handwritten New Testament documents available for study. They include more than 5,300 in the original Greek language, more than 8,000 in Latin, and more than 10,000 in other languages and lectionaries.

You might be surprised to learn that only 10 handwritten copies of *Caesar's War Commentaries* have ever been found—and only seven copies of one of Plato's well-known works. Yet, finding just a few copies is the norm. The New Testament is an exception in that over 14,500 handwritten copies have been found.[2]

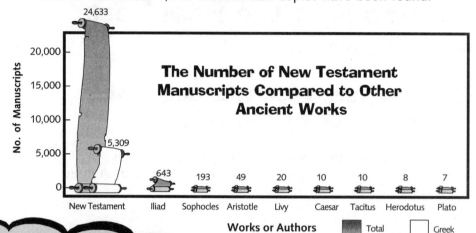

The Number of New Testament Manuscripts Compared to Other Ancient Works

THINK ABOUT IT

The number of New Testament copies is awesome. It passes the first part of the test with flying colors!

In the above graph, which ancient writing has the fewest handwritten copies?

Which has the most? _____

Which ancient work has the closest number of copies to the New Testament?

Moving on to the next step:

The earlier the date of a manuscript, the more accurate it is likely to be.

Most people I talk to are surprised to discover that there are no preserved copies of any classical Greek work for several hundred years after the date of the original writing.

– Dr. Don

2. How early were the manuscripts written?

Learning the date that a manuscript copy was written helps determine the accuracy. The larger the gap between the time a copy was made and the time originals were composed, the more likely it is that errors have accumulated.

The gap between the original writing of *Caesar's War Commentaries* and the date of the earliest copy we have now is about average. It was written about 50 B.C., but no copies dated before the ninth century have been found. That's a gap of over 900 years!

Check out the chart on the next page. Which ancient work has the shortest time span between the original writing and the earliest available copy?

But what about the New Testament? Those who study ancient documents generally agree that the original 27 books of the New Testament were written between about A.D. 47 and A.D. 100. Complete Gospels have been found, like the Beatty and Bodmer Papyri, that date less than 100 years after the time the originals were written. This is a shorter time span than any other ancient writing.

The Time Interval Between the Date of Writing and the Earliest Known Manuscript of the New Testament Compared to Other Ancient Works

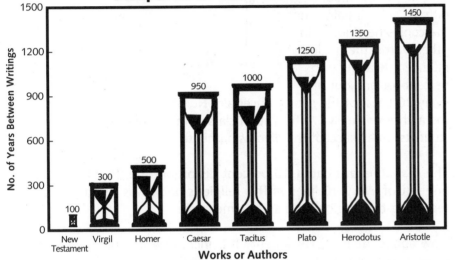

As a skeptic, I was sure that the stories of Jesus were not accurate. But when I learned how early the manuscript copies were, I had to ask myself, "When could the records about Jesus have changed?" Realizing there is a continuous chain of handwritten copies from the time of the originals in Jesus' generation to the time of the 15th century printing press, I had to conclude that the New Testament of today has not changed very much since the eyewitnesses wrote it 2,000 years ago.

– Dr. Don

But that's not all. Fragments of manuscripts have been found that date between A.D. 50 and A.D. 70. Since Jesus lived until A.D. 30, these copies were made by people who lived in the same generation as he did. To get copies this early, the original New Testament writings must have been written earlier. It is clear that the gospel information about Jesus was written by his contemporaries—people who heard Jesus personally or talked with those who did.

In the second step of the integrity test, the New Testament again outshines all other ancient writings!

3. How accurately were the handwritten manuscripts copied?

Now we're ready for the final part of the integrity test. Having so many copies of the New Testament is helpful. They can be compared to see how much change occurred as the result of copying errors. Dr. Bruce Metzger, a professor at Princeton University, studied the rate of distortion among the manuscripts of three famous ancient religious works.[3] They included the Christian New Testament, the *Iliad* (a religious work of the ancient Greeks), and the *Mahabharata* (a religious book of Hinduism).

DEFINITION

Distortion rate: The degree of change that occurs due to errors in hand-copying a manuscript.

MAGDALEN PAPYRUS

The Magdalen Papyrus, dated between A.D. 50 and 70, contains a few verses of the gospel of Matthew. Some fragments of Mark and Luke date in the late A.D. 60's, and one of John (the John Rylands Papyrus) from about A.D. 120.[4]

To make his task easier, Metzger divided the three works into lines of 10 words each. They varied in length from 15,600 lines for the *Iliad*, 20,000 for the New Testament and 250,000 for the *Mahabharata*. He then counted all the differences in the various manuscripts that would affect the reader's understanding.

OUTSIDE SOURCES

Other ancient writings confirm the accuracy of the New Testament. During the 300 years after Jesus lived, more than 36,000 quotations from the New Testament were included in other people's books and letters. In fact, the New Testament was quoted so often that it could almost be entirely reconstructed from these other sources.

Dr. Metzger's research results

Dr. Metzger reported that 764 lines of the *Iliad* differed substantially among the copies he studied. In other words, the original intended meaning of 5 percent (or one out of

A Comparison of the Rate of Distortion of Manuscripts Due to Copying Errors

New Testament	Iliad	Mahabharata
0.2	4.9	10.3

every 20 lines) of the *Iliad* is uncertain. No one knows for sure what the author originally wrote. Yet, in classroom settings instructors and students usually accept the *Iliad* as authentic.

The *Mahabharata* had a 10 percent distortion rate. In other words, one out of every 10 lines of this religious book was "up for grabs" regarding the original text and its meaning.

How about the New Testament? It is incredibly accurate compared to all other writings. In comparing the 24,000 plus copies available, only 40 lines of the entire work are changed in a way that affects understanding of the meaning. That's only one-fifth of 1 percent (0.2%) of the lines. That's 25 times more accurately copied than the *Iliad*. According to scholars, the few differences among the handwritten New Testament manuscripts are relatively minor. They don't raise significant questions about historic facts, and they don't affect any basic Christian teachings.

At this point, I suspect that some of you are thinking as I did during my own faith search: "Okay, the New Testament was written by eyewitnesses and copied accurately over the years, but maybe the stories about Jesus' birth, death, crucifixion and resurrection are fabrications, like fairy tales." I'm glad I continued my search.
— Dr. Don

Where does our search take us now?

The scientific evidence clearly shows that the New Testament record of Jesus' life that we hold in our hands today is essentially the same as the writers wrote it in the first century. This can be said of no other ancient book in the world.

But how can we know whether a written account is based on reality? Ancient writings might be authentic and have integrity, but be based simply on stories rather than things that actually happened. The next step is to look at the scientific evidence from archaeology. This will show if New Testament accounts are true to historical facts.

The Real Jesus of History

unit two - day three

Did the people in the New Testament really exist and did the events really happen?

We've established that the New Testament is authentic and has integrity. In other words, it was written by people who lived at the same time as Jesus, and their writings were accurately copied through the centuries. Therefore, the New Testament we have today is the same as eyewitnesses wrote it 2,000 years ago.

As the judge and jury, our next task is to evaluate the historical reliability of New Testament writings. In order to do this, we'll follow the method most often used by literary scholars. First, we'll look for any outside sources (like archaeology) to see if they confirm that the people, places and events of the New Testament were part of history. Then we'll learn as much as we can about the New Testament writings and their authors by looking at what is known about the history of that time.

Was Jesus a real person?

Most of the information that is known about Jesus is in the four Gospels of the New Testament—Matthew, Mark, Luke and John. While these are excellent sources, I want to see if writings outside the New Testament also mention that a man called Jesus of Nazareth lived when the Bible says he did.

Let's start our examination of this evidence by looking at the works of Josephus, a Jew, and Tacitus, a Roman. These men are accepted as reliable reporters by modern historians. Josephus mentions Jesus several times.[1] He notes Jesus' role as a religious teacher and his death by crucifixion. Tacitus tells us that Jesus lived during the time the New Testament claims he did and that he was referred to as the "Christ" by his followers.[2]

Did the people in the New Testament really exist and did the events really happen?

How do we know the stories are true?

ANCIENT REPORTERS

Josephus and Tacitus were respected reporters of ancient events. They mentioned Jesus in their writings of about A.D. 100.

The Evidence of Archaeology

Scientific archaeology is only about a century and a half old. The techniques used today were first pioneered by British scientists and have led to a revolution of knowledge about ancient times. In the past, critics have questioned the historical accuracy of parts of the New Testament. However, as more dirt is overturned by archeologists, more evidence is being found to support the New Testament. Today, plenty of data is available to check the historical veracity (truthfulness) of the New Testament.

Neither Tacitus or Josephus were followers of Jesus. There would have been no reason for them to include information about a Jesus of Nazareth who was called the Christ and who was crucified by Pontius Pilate if he didn't exist. Their works and many others confirm that Jesus was a real historical figure whose interactions with people led to the establishment of the Christian faith.

THINK ABOUT IT

Why does the fact that Josephus and Tacitus were not followers of Jesus make their statements about him more credible than if they had been followers?

_____

_____

_____

ABOUT LUKE

Luke was a physician and a traveling companion of the apostle Paul. He wrote two books of the New Testament—Luke and Acts—in which he was careful to include historical details.

DISCOVERIES

Excavation of the site of ancient Caesarea, the city where Pontius Pilate lived, uncovered a 2 x 3 foot cornerstone from the first century with the inscription, "Pontius Pilate, the Prefect of Judea, has dedicated to the people of Caesarea a temple in honor of Tiberius."[6]

What about the PEOPLE in the Gospels?

There are many opportunities to test the accuracy of the New Testament writings by comparing details with data uncovered by archeologists. Expert literary scholars also help by comparing writings of the New Testament to other historical documents to see whether the timing of events and other details are consistent.

Luke mentions the Roman governor Pontius Pilate and the Caesars Augustus and Tiberius who were Roman emperors during Jesus' time.[3] Historians have confirmed that these are real people who lived during the time period the New Testament claims they did.

Luke also mentions Caiaphas as the high priest who presided over the trial of Jesus.[4] Recently, during road construction in Jerusalem, heavy equipment broke through the roof of a limestone cave used for burial in the first century. Inside the cave was a sculptured bone box, or ossuary, with the name of the occupant engraved on the side. It was "Joseph Caiaphas," the same high priest mentioned by Luke.[5]

During the apostle Paul's second missionary journey, he visited the city of Thessalonica. Luke refers to the city judges there as "politarchs."[7] Since this title does not appear in any other ancient literature, for many years critics assumed that Luke had made up the term. But in the late 19th century, archaeologist William Ramsay uncovered the stone archway of the gate into the city of Thessalonica in Paul's time. Above the Greek names engraved on the archway was the title "politarchs."[8] Since then, at least 19 additional inscriptions of this title have been found by archaeologists that prove Luke was correct.[9]

POLITARCHS
"Politarch" was the title applied to magistrates in some Macedonian towns during Paul's time.

REAL PEOPLE
Pontius Pilate, Caesar Augustus and Caesar Tiberius are familiar names today, and are mentioned by Luke and other New Testament writers

The Jewish high priest Caiaphas, whom the Gospels claim tried Jesus, has been confirmed as real by recent discoveries.

An Archaeologist's Testimony
William Ramsay, classical scholar and archaeologist at Oxford University, spent his life researching the history recorded in the Bible. He started his work as a nonbeliever, but was so impressed by what he discovered during his studies that he became a believer. In fact, Ramsay considered the physician Luke's writing as "unsurpassed in respect of its trustworthiness," and he considered Luke among "the very greatest of historians." [10]

BIBLE DISCOVERY

Read Luke 1:1-4 and 3:1-2. Note the care he took to be accurate and detailed in his reports.

1. Where did Luke get the information he wrote about Jesus and why did he write it?_____

2. How did Luke identify the year in which John the Baptist preached in the desert?_____

3. Who was governor of Judea at the time?_____

A writer who thus relates his story to the wider context of world history is courting trouble if he is not careful; he affords his critical readers so many opportunities for testing his accuracy. Luke takes this risk and stands the test admirably.
– F. F. Bruce, The New Testament Documents: Are They Reliable? p.82

Real Places & Events
in the Bible
unit two - day four

PLACES mentioned in the Bible

Some of the places mentioned in the Bible are still present today and obviously real—like Jerusalem, Egypt and the Sea of Galilee. Others have been verified as historical only after excavation of ancient ruins—Capernaum and Herodean are examples.

Facts about the Old Testament are also being confirmed. **Sodom** and **Gomorrah** were cities of the Old Testament. According to the book of Genesis, the people in them were so wicked that God destroyed the entire cities.[1] For centuries, critics assumed that Bible writers had added stories about them to teach a moral lesson. But recent excavation of the ancient city of Ebla in northern Syria uncovered a library containing more than 20,000 stone tablets.[2] These tablets (from 2000-2500 B.C.) recorded city business transactions and included a reference to the cities of Sodom and Gomorrah as trading partners. They were real cities after all!

Until this century, the **Hittite** people were totally unknown except for references to them in the Old Testament. Critics said that they were fictitious or given a wrong name by the Bible writers. But twentieth century archaeologists have confirmed that the Hittites were real people who once occupied much of modern Turkey.[3]

PALESTINE IN JESUS' DAY

PHOENICIA

Tyre •   • Caesarea-Philippi

GALILEE
Chorazin •
Capernaum • • Bethsaida
Gennesaret • • Gergesa
Cana •   SEA OF
Nazareth •   GALILEE
Nain •   • Gadara

JORDAN RIVER

DECAPOLIS

SAMARIA

Sychar •

PEREA

Jericho •
Emmaus •   Jerusalem • • Bethany
Bethlehem •

JUDEA   DEAD SEA

EVENTS mentioned in the Bible

<u>Facts about the Roman census:</u> The Gospel of Luke states that Joseph and Mary traveled to Bethlehem to be registered for a Roman census.[4] Historical documents confirm that the Roman Empire conducted a census every 14 years beginning with Augustus.[5] The journey of Joseph and Mary to Bethlehem to be registered (where Mary gave birth to Jesus) coincides with one of these Roman censuses.

<u>Facts about legal proceedings during Jesus' time:</u> The way the New Testament describes the legal proceedings against Jesus and the apostle Paul correspond with what we know of Roman practices in that time.[6] Based on our growing knowledge of that era, historians also highly praise Luke for his accuracy in describing the setting and the atmosphere at trials and other events in Jesus' day.

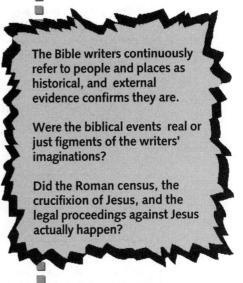

The Bible writers continuously refer to people and places as historical, and external evidence confirms they are.

Were the biblical events real or just figments of the writers' imaginations?

Did the Roman census, the crucifixion of Jesus, and the legal proceedings against Jesus actually happen?

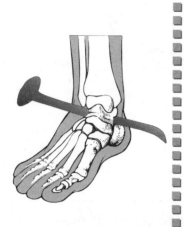

DEFINITION
Crucifixion: The practice of hanging criminals on a cross until they died of asphyxiation due to sheer physical exhaustion.

Facts about Jesus' crucifixion: The gospel writers tell us that Jesus was put to death by crucifixion. The Bible tells us that Jesus was nailed to the cross in the city of Jerusalem. At one time, the only information that we had about the practice of crucifixion came from Roman documents. The Romans talked about tying, rather than nailing, victims to the cross. Therefore, critics claimed that the Gospel writers must have embellished their stories with inaccurate details. Some suggested that crucifixions never occurred in Palestine.

However, a recent archaeological discovery supports the Biblical crucifixion account.[7] From a tomb near Jerusalem, a scientist discovered the skeleton of a crucifixion victim—the only one ever found. It was of a man in his mid-to-late 20s. He had a 7$\frac{1}{2}$-inch-long nail through his feet. The man's crucifixion was dated at A.D. 42—just 12 years after the approximate date that Jesus was crucified. This verifies that crucifixions did take place in Jerusalem and that nails were actually used to fasten victims to the cross.

According to researchers, the calf bones of the uncovered skeleton were also "brutally fractured" in a way that suggests they were broken by "a single, strong blow." This is amazing evidence. It supports another practice of crucifixion described in the gospel of John in the New Testament.

The Romans made it a practice to let the crucified person die slowly of sheer physical exhaustion, which led to suffocation. This could take a matter of days. However, Jewish laws required burial of the crucified person on the day of execution. By breaking the legs of the crucified person (making it impossible for the victim to raise the body to breathe) the Jews could hasten death and bury the body before nightfall. This practice, described in the Gospels in reference to the two thieves who were crucified next to Jesus, has now been verified by archaeology.[8]

BIBLE DISCOVERY

Take a break here and look up John 19:32-33. Write out the verse as it describes Jesus' crucifixion:

_____

_____

_____

_____

Over the years, we can see a pattern. The more archaeological information found, the more evidence we have to support the historical accuracy of people, places and events that are discussed in the Bible.

Testimonies from scholars

Many international scholars also judge the New Testament to be historically accurate.

"...archaeological work has unquestionably strengthened confidence in the reliability of the scriptural record. More than one archaeologist has found his respect for the Bible increased by the experience of excavation in Palestine."[9]

—Millar Burrows, Yale University

Here Dr. Burrows gives a real challenge to those who desire evidence for the truthfulness of the New Testament—grab a spade and check it out. You'll become convinced.

"Discovery after discovery has established the accuracy of innumerable details, and has brought increased recognition to the value of the Bible as a source of history."

— William Albright, Johns Hopkins University archaeologist

"Archaeology has not yet said its last word, but the results already achieved confirm what faith would suggest, that the Bible can do nothing but gain from an increase in knowledge."[10]

–Frederic Kenyon

Note: Kenyon was considered a foremost authority in this field more than 50 years ago. More recently, Kitchen, another authority, affirmed that Kenyon was right when he said: "Continuing discoveries and work of the intervening decades have not changed, merely enhanced, the truth of his judgment."[11]

Judging the Real Facts

unit two - day five

Imagine for a moment that someone asks me to write the life story of former president John F. Kennedy. But I didn't know him personally nor do I have time to research the facts of his life. What am I to do? Since he was assassinated more than 35 years ago, I decide to just make up some things and hope that no one will remember the truth.

After some months, I publish my biography of JFK. My opening sentence reads: "John F. Kennedy, though born into a very poor family, nevertheless fulfilled the American dream by becoming his nation's president." Is there anyone alive today who might know that the Kennedys were actually very wealthy? Of course! Thirty-five years is not enough time to erase the memory of the facts.

Later in JFK's biography, I claim that he walked on water, healed the sick in front of crowds, raised the dead, and fed 5,000 people with 25 hamburgers and 10 packs of French fries. And after his death, he was resurrected and ascended to heaven in front of over 500 eyewitnesses. This would make a great tabloid headline, but would Americans today really believe this? No!

Why? Because 35 years later is too close to JFK's time for people to fall for such lies. Only after enough time has passed that everyone who knew the Kennedys has died would you have a chance of passing off such stories as true.

How would people respond if someone wrote a book claiming that John F. Kennedy did the things Jesus did?

Eyewitnesses of Jesus

Jesus preached for three and one-half years throughout Israel. At the end of that time, in about A.D. 30, he was crucified at the Feast of Passover in the city

> "Men of Israel, hear these words: Jesus of Nazareth, a Man attested by God to you by miracles, wonders, and signs which God did through Him in your midst, as you yourselves also know." Peter goes on to say "This Jesus God has raised up, of which we are all witnesses."
>
> Acts 2:22,32 (NKJ)

of Jerusalem. About 50 days after Jesus died, at the Feast of Pentecost, the apostle Peter stood in Jerusalem and spoke to the crowds about him.[1]

In my youth, I thought that the New Testament stories about Jesus were legends developed long after he was gone. So, I reasoned: Why would anyone believe 2,000-year-old stories written by people who were not even around in Jesus' lifetime? Since then I've learned how mistaken I was.

– Dr. Don

PAUL

Paul was a Jewish enemy of Jesus before he was converted to Christianity. After his conversion, he put his life on the line to testify before Roman officials and King Agrippa that the historical evidence for Jesus' life was public knowledge and true.

Peter claimed Jesus did miraculous things—like walking on water, healing the sick in front of crowds, raising the dead, and feeding 5,000 people with five barley loaves and two fish. If Jesus healed *your* mother from a terminal disease or raised *your* brother from the dead, would you remember? Of course! You would never forget.

Many people hostile to Christians were among the crowd who heard Peter speak. Yet there is no indication that anyone challenged his statements about Jesus' miracles, wonders and signs. Furthermore, when Peter reminded the people of Jesus' miracles and resurrection, 3,000 Jewish people responded by becoming Christians.[2] That wouldn't happen if they knew that Jesus was a fraud or a product of Peter's imagination. And if Peter was lying about Jesus, he was surely smart enough to leave Jerusalem, cross the Mediterranean, and go where people had no firsthand knowledge of Jesus.

BIBLE DISCOVERY

Look up Acts 2:22,32 in your Bible, which records Peter's message to the people of Jerusalem, and answer the following questions:

1. To whom is Peter speaking?_____

2. How does he describe Jesus?_____

3. What does he say God did?_____

4. Who does he say knows about these events?_____

5. Who does he say saw the resurrection of Jesus?_____

We've examined the evidence for the second condition to test the "God hypothesis"—the need for a trustworthy first-century historical record about Jesus. Here is what we've discovered:

1. The evidence of early manuscripts shows that what we read in the New Testament today is the same information recorded by eyewitnesses of Jesus.

2. The science of archaeology and other studies show that the information about Jesus in the New Testament is historically accurate.

It is reasonable and logical to conclude from this evidence that the New Testament is the most authentic and historically reliable writing of ancient times.

You be the judge

The earliest Christian converts were Jews who witnessed the things that Jesus did. It is significant that Christian teaching was believed by people in Jerusalem who were in the best position to know whether or not it was true.

Legends are not believed as true within the same generation as the events and persons themselves. Remember that we couldn't fabricate JFK's life story in our generation, even though he lived more than 35 years ago. The New Testament was written and published within 25 years after Jesus' death and resurrection. After this length of time, would people be around who knew the facts about Jesus? Of course! How could Christianity possibly have succeeded among the eyewitnesses in Israel if it were not true?

Even after I found out that the New Testament we have today is authentic and historically accurate, I wondered how I could really know that Jesus was God. What evidence could Jesus present to make his school classmates believe that? Why would we believe it today? In the next step of my faith search, I discovered what Jesus said about himself and what he did to back up his claim. I'm looking forward to sharing what I learned with you in the next section.

– Dr. Don

unit three

Searching for the Real Jesus

By the Way... I'm God

unit three - day one

How would you react if one of your friends claimed to be God?

Let's pretend for a moment. Rob and I grew up together, were in the same grade at school and shared a lot of good times. I went my separate way after high school and lost touch with Rob for a number of years. So I am quite excited when I receive a notice that my class is having its 10-year reunion and Rob is on the list of those who are going to be there.

The occasion is awesome. It's great to hear what former classmates have done since high school. When it's time for Rob to share, he makes sure everyone can see him and announces: "There is something I've been anticipating telling you for some time now—I'm God!"

A similar scenario really occurred nearly 2,000 years ago. Jesus was born into a Jewish family in the small town of Nazareth in Israel, a remote province of the Roman empire. He played with the neighbor kids outside his dad's carpenter shop, and went to the synagogue school with his friends. After school, he went his separate way for a few years. Then, when he was about 30 years old, he stood up in the synagogue of his home town and announced that he was the Christ, the Son of God.

NEARLY 2,000 YEARS AGO A SMALL-TOWN BOY CLAIMED TO BE GOD

Anyone making claims like that—today or 2,000 years ago—had better have some pretty powerful reasons to back them up if they are serious. In our continuing faith search, we'll first investigate what Jesus said about himself and what he did to back it up. Then, based on the evidence of our search, we will ask, "Who is Jesus?" As a member of the jury, you will need to decide and declare a verdict.

A SHOCKER

The Jews of Jesus' day rarely spoke the name of God for fear that they may be judged for defiling its holiness with their unclean lips. Jesus not only spoke God's name, he claimed it as his own!

FOR MEMORY

Jesus did many other miraculous signs in the presence of his disciples, which are not recorded in this book. But these are written that you may believe that Jesus is the Christ, the Son of God, and that by believing you may have life in his name.

John 20:30-31

If someone I knew claimed to be God, my first response would likely be, "Yeah, right. And I'm Superman!" I think you'd agree that an announcement such as Rob's would be the talk of a reunion. Some might laugh, assuming it was a joke. Others might be shocked, thinking that he had "lost it." As a friend, I might try talking to Rob alone to find out what is going on.

– Dr. Don

JEWISH BELIEFS

The Jews in Jesus' day believed the prophecy that Jesus read from Isaiah would be fulfilled by the Messiah when he came. Read Isaiah 61:1, 2a and Isaiah 9:6. Note that in 9:6 the Messiah is referred to as "Mighty God" and the "Eternal Father."

A field trip with eyewitnesses

As a biology professor, my professional expertise was ecology. I often took my students on nature field trips so they could experience the lecture subject firsthand. It was a great time. So, why not take a field trip through the gospel accounts of Jesus in order to hear what the eyewitnesses heard, and see what they saw—experience if first hand.

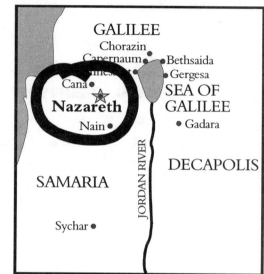

Jesus said: I am the CHRIST (Messiah)[1]

Our field trip starts in Nazareth at a gathering in the local synagogue where Jesus is teaching. Peter and John, later writers of the New Testament, sit beside us. As we listen, Jesus reads from the Old Testament a familiar prophecy from the book of Isaiah. It tells about the coming of the Messiah. He concludes his reading by saying, "Today this Scripture has been fulfilled in your hearing." In other words, Jesus said, "Here I am, ready or not!"

Since Jesus is quoting the Old Testament prophet Isaiah, he undoubtedly knows that in the same book, Isaiah calls Messiah the "Eternal Father," a reference to God.[2] Therefore, when he says Scripture has been fulfilled, he is claiming to be a divine Messiah. The people around us assume that, too. Some express shock saying, "Isn't this Joseph's son?"

Just as my friends would expect Rob to back up his claims, people around us expect Jesus to back up his claim to be the Messiah. Jesus anticipates this and says, "No doubt you will quote this proverb to me, 'Physician, heal yourself.'" This is the same as saying, "Prove it!"

The people are skeptical and at this point they reject Jesus' claim. Who is right—Jesus or the people? We'll be looking at the evidence later in our field trip, but for now, let's continue to follow Jesus and listen to what else he says.

Jesus said: I am the LORD God[3]

We catch up with Jesus as he addresses a group of Pharisees. This time Matthew, a tax collector (and later a New Testament writer), is among them. The Pharisees know from the Old Testament prophecies that the Messiah will be a descendent of King David. So when Jesus asks, "What do you think about the Christ, whose son is he?", the

WHAT DO YOU KNOW?

Fill in the blanks:

1. When Jesus said that Scripture has been fulfilled in his coming, he is claiming to be the _____ whose coming was prophesied by _____ in the Old Testament.

2. The Jews of Jesus' day believed that the Messiah had only a _____ nature.

3. Jesus corrected the Pharisees, explaining the Messiah was both man and _____.

Pharisees answer: "The son of David." By that they mean that the Messiah has a human nature only—like you and me.

Jesus responds with another question: "Then how does David in the Spirit call him 'Lord' saying 'The Lord said to my Lord...'?" Jesus has just quoted the words of David from Psalm 110:1. He goes on to ask: "If David then calls him [the Messiah] 'Lord,' how is he his son?"

His question leaves the **Pharisees** speechless. Why? They're surprised that Jesus is correcting an error in their teaching. He's telling them that David used the name of God to refer to the Messiah.

Jesus said: I am the I AM[4]

Jesus isn't always subtle in his claims to be God. Later the Jewish leaders ask him point blank, "Whom do you make yourself out to be?" Jesus responds, "Truly, truly, I say to you, before Abraham was born, I AM." By saying this, Jesus is claiming to have lived before Abraham who had lived about 2,000 years earlier. In fact, by referring to himself as "I AM," he is saying he had no beginning—he always existed.

The people around us are shocked. They know that "I AM" is one of the names for God in the Old Testament.[5] Therefore, the Jewish leaders see Jesus' statement as blasphemy. They're so upset they begin picking up stones to fling at him. Jesus and his followers make a hasty retreat to keep from being stoned to death.

Jesus said: I am ONE with the Father[6]

As we follow Jesus, we hear people continue to ask about his identity. At the winter Feast of Dedication in Jerusalem, he is asked, "How long will you keep us in suspense? If you are the Christ, tell us plainly." Jesus responds, "I told you, and you do not believe... ."

He goes on to say, "I and the Father are one." The crowd is getting ready to stone him again. When Jesus asks why, they say "...for blasphemy; and because you, being a man, make yourself out to be God."

JESUS' POINT

The point of Jesus' question: "Then how does David in the Spirit call him 'Lord' saying "The Lord said to my Lord..." is this: If David refers to the Messiah (his physical descendant) by the name of God, the Pharisees should teach that the Messiah is God. The actual words of David in Psalm 110:1 were, "*Yahweh* said to *Adonai.*" Both names refer to God, but David applies *Adonai* to his descendant who would be the Messiah. Jesus wanted the Pharisees to understand that, as the Messiah, he was both man and God.

EQUAL TO GOD?

When Jesus said: " I am ONE with the Father" (John 10:30-33), the Jewish leaders knew that he was claiming to be equal to (of the same essence as) God.

ETERNAL LIFE

Jesus said he can give eternal life (John 11:25-26). Imagine walking around a busy shopping mall and asking people if they would like to live forever—then telling them that you were the one who could grant them eternal life!

Jesus said: I can give you eternal life[7]

On still another leg of our field trip, we are with Jesus when he talks to Martha and Mary right after their brother Lazarus died. Jesus tells these two women, "I am the resurrection and the life; he who believes in me shall live even if he dies, and everyone who lives and believes in me shall never die." Later he tells someone else that he can give eternal life to anyone he wants to.

Through the ears of the eyewitnesses, we heard Jesus claim to be God on many occasions. If we were to say much of what Jesus said, we would be considered candidates for psychiatric treatment. Actually, Jesus died for what he said. Throughout history people have been sentenced for what they do, that is, for some crime committed. But Jesus was crucified for **who** he claimed to be: "He ought to die because he made himself out to be the Son of God."[8]

BIBLE DISCOVERY

Read these additional eyewitness passages to check out some of Jesus' other claims for yourself, and fill in the blanks accordingly:

1. John 8:23-24 "You are from below, I am from _____; you are of this world; I am _____ of this world."

2. Matthew 28:18 "All _____ has been given to me in _____ and on _____."

3. John 8:46 He claimed to be without _____.

4. John 14:6 He claimed to be the only _____.

A summary of Jesus' claims

1. He said that he is the Messiah (Christ) and the "Mighty God" and "Everlasting Father."
2. He said that he is the Lord God (Adonai).
3. He said that he is the "I AM" meaning God the Eternal One.
4. He said that he is "one with the Father" meaning equal.
5. He said that he is "from above and not of the world."
6. He said that he can give eternal life to anyone.
7. He said that he has "all authority in heaven and on earth."
8. He said that he is without sin.
9. He said that he is the exclusive (only) way to God.

Were Jesus' claims more than a delusion or an empty boast? In the next part of our field trip, we'll consider this question.

Jesus...

Doing What God Does

unit three - day two

Did Jesus really do anything that showed he was God?

The more time people spent with Jesus, the more certain they were that his claims to be God were true. Why? Let's continue our field trip and find out. We'll see for ourselves what caused many people to change their minds about Jesus. For approximately two years after Jesus first claimed to be God in his hometown of Nazareth, Luke recorded his actions. Let's view Jesus' actions through the eyes of those who were actually there.

Jesus demonstrates his right and ability to forgive sins

One day as he [Jesus] was teaching...Some men came carrying a paralytic on a mat....When Jesus saw their faith, he said, "Friend, your sins are forgiven." The Pharisees and the teachers of the law began thinking to themselves, "Who is this fellow who speaks blasphemy? Who can forgive sins but God alone?"...Jesus knew what they were thinking... "But that you may know that the Son of Man has authority on earth to forgive sins...." He said to the paralyzed man, "I tell you, get up, take your mat and go home." Immediately he stood up in front of them, took what he had been lying on and went home....
Luke 5:17-26

Our first stop is Capernaum, a city on the northwest shoreline of the Sea of Galilee. Jesus has come here following his announcement at the synagogue in Nazareth. We're in the apostle Peter's home. It is filled with many of Israel's most capable religious leaders—**Pharisees** and **scribes**. Four men carrying a paralyzed friend on a stretcher can't make their way through the crowd to get to Jesus.[2] We watch as they do a desperate thing—

DEFINITION
Pharisees: Jewish religious teachers.

Scribes: The lawyers of biblical times.

A TOP-NOTCH REPORTER
Remember that Luke was a physician who has been acclaimed by many prominent historians for his accuracy in reporting accurate details. He was a contemporary of Jesus and his disciples.

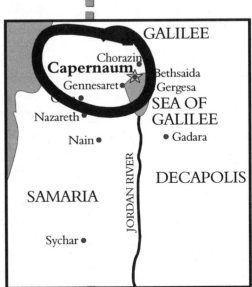

they break a hole in the roof and lower their friend down to Jesus. Jesus realizes the men want him to heal their friend. He responds by saying, "Friend, your sins are forgiven." The men on the roof, look at each other in bewilderment. Doesn't Jesus notice that their friend is paralyzed? They expected healing for him—not forgiveness.

Meanwhile, we hear comments from the lawyers and Pharisees such as: "Who is this fellow who speaks blasphemies? Who can forgive sins, but God alone?"

THINK ABOUT IT

Why were the Pharisees angry with Jesus when he told the paralytic that his sins were forgiven?

_____

_____

Why did Jesus choose to heal somebody in order to prove that he had the ability to forgive sins?

_____

Relating the story of the paralytic to real life

An illustration might help to explain why the religious leaders were so upset by Jesus' statement. Pretend that you have been assigned a research paper that you work for hours to complete. Before you turn it in, a guy named Bob steals it from your locker, puts his name on it, and turns it in for credit. You get an "F" for not turning the assignment in on time. Later you overhear Cindy, another student, telling Bob she forgives him for stealing your paper. Would you be okay with that?

I doubt it. You'd likely be upset thinking that Cindy had no right to forgive Bob. He never did anything to her. After all, it was **your** assignment that had been stolen. **You** are the only one who can do the forgiving.

Like Cindy, Jesus is the third party. He had probably never seen this paralyzed man before. This man had never done anything to Jesus. If he had sinned, it was against God. How can Jesus take the position and the right of God to offer the man forgiveness? To the Pharisees and lawyers, Jesus was committing blasphemy by acting as if he were God. Besides, in their minds, Jesus' promise of forgiveness was empty because they didn't believe that he took away the man's sin.

How could Jesus demonstrate that he did? After announcing that he will prove that he has authority on earth to forgive sins, he says to the paralytic, "I say to you, rise, and take up your stretcher and go home." The man is instantly healed. Everyone is astonished. But how did that prove that Jesus had taken away the man's sin?

The ancient Jewish view of sin

Jewish people in Jesus' time believed that sin directly results in judgment or other consequences. For example, if I were hanging out with a group of Pharisees and fell down a flight of stairs, they would gather around and ask me what sin I had committed recently to cause this judgment. On one occasion, Jesus' own disciples stopped him in front of a man who had been born blind and asked, "Rabbi, who sinned, this man or his parents, that he was born blind?" [1]

Because of their beliefs, when the paralyzed man appeared on his stretcher, the Jewish religious authorities saw his disease as a consequence of some sin he had committed. This was an opportunity for Jesus to demonstrate the removal of the man's sin by healing him. If sin is causing paralysis, then healing the paralysis will show that the sin is removed. Jesus had just given them a good reason to believe that he is God.

As an interesting side note, other teachings by Jesus indicate that he did not share the Pharisees' simplistic belief that misfortunes are always the direct consequences of sin (see Luke 13:1-5). But in this case, Jesus relied on their beliefs to demonstrate his authority as God.

– Dr. Don

Presence of Sin

⬇

Leads to

⬇

Consequence of Sin

Removal of the Sin that caused it

⬆

Proves

⬆

Removal of the Consequence of Sin

 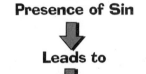 **BIBLE DISCOVERY**

Read for yourself the details of Luke's account in Luke 5:17-26.

1. Explain why you think the religious leaders were so upset when Jesus told the paralytic that his sins were forgiven.

_____

2. Is that the same reaction you would have had in a similar situation? Explain.

_____

Jesus
Demonstrates Real Authority
unit three - day three

Soon afterward, Jesus went to a town called Nain, and his disciples and a large crowd went with him. As he approached the town gate, a dead person was being carried out...Then he went up and touched the coffin, and those carrying it stood still. He said, "Young man, I say to you, get up!"...They were all filled with awe and praised God.   Luke 7:11-16

Jesus demonstrates authority over death[1]

Moving along on our field trip, we approach the southern Galilean city of Nain. Here we meet a funeral procession taking a widow's only son to burial. Instead of stepping aside and letting them pass, Jesus approaches the mourning widow with compassion and says, "Do not weep." He then stops the procession, goes up and touches the coffin, and says to the dead son, "Young man, I say to you, arise!"

Amazingly, the young man's head lifts up, he sits and then stands—and he speaks! Now WE are looking for a place to sit down. The crowd draws back in fear. All around there are comments such as: "A great prophet has arisen among us!" and "God has visited his people!" It's getting harder and harder for people to think of Jesus as just a carpenter's son.

Jesus demonstrates authority over the laws of nature

One day Jesus said to his disciples, "Let's go over to the other side of the lake." So they got into a boat and set out... . A squall came down on the lake, so that the boat was being swamped... . He got up and rebuked the wind and the raging waters; the storm subsided and all was calm.   Luke 8:22-25

To get to the next destination, we need to cross the Sea of Galilee. We get into a fishing boat equipped with a sleeper, and Jesus lies down for a nap. Some distance out on the lake, a sudden, severe wind rocks us, and we all panic—we're going down!

Now, I must admit, if I had really been a casual observer or a curious follower of Jesus the day that Jesus starting talking to a dead man, I'd be embarrassed. Jesus is making a scene. And to tell a dead man to get up out of his coffin—well, it just isn't going to happen. But it did!

Jesus had compassion for the widow, and raised her son from the dead. Many others present that day had compassion too, but all they could do was weep. The difference between the two is immense. The only way this event would not impact my view of Jesus as God is if I denied that it ever happened. But on what basis? I've already discovered that the books of the New Testament are reliable records of eyewitnesses.

– Dr. Don

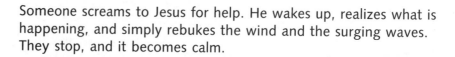

Someone screams to Jesus for help. He wakes up, realizes what is happening, and simply rebukes the wind and the surging waves. They stop, and it becomes calm.

Jesus' control over the laws of nature is so instant and decisive that his disciples ask in astonishment, "Who then is this, that he commands even the winds and the water, and they obey him?" Good question.

Jesus demonstrates authority over the spirit world

In the synagogue there was a man possessed by a demon, an evil spirit. He cried out at the top of his voice... . "Be quiet!" Jesus said sternly. "Come out of him!" Then the demon threw the man down before them all and came out... .   Luke 4:33-36.

When we get to the other side of the lake, we follow Jesus to the city of Capernaum. As we enter the city, Jesus is confronted by a man who the local people know is possessed by demonic spirits. Without hesitation, Jesus commands the spirits to "Be quiet and come out of him!" They immediately obey, and the man becomes calm and in his right mind.

Who would have such authority? There are only two choices. The Jewish religious leaders realize that Jesus is either a ruling demon himself, or he is God. They accuse him of being the first. Other people begin asking, "What is this message?" or "What does this show us about who he is?" They recognized such authority was evidence that he was more than a carpenter's son.

How does Jesus explain his own actions?

Jesus intended to give good reasons for people to believe in him. He told his followers: "Do not believe me unless I do what my Father does. But if I do it, even though you do not believe me, believe the miracles..."[2] That's what we have been observing—the miracles of Jesus.

Jesus once claimed that he had all authority in heaven and earth. In a three-and-a-half-year time of history, he proved it. He demonstrated before eyewitnesses his authority over everything that exists. No wonder Jesus caused such a revolution in the lives of his disciples!

On our field trip, we had the opportunity to hear what Jesus said about himself, and see what he could do. As a member of the jury, your job now is to come to a verdict concerning who he is.

Do you know anyone else who has authority and power over sin and sickness, death, the laws of nature and the spirit world? Who do you say that Jesus is? In the next chapter, we'll examine all the possible options.

If Jesus were a demon, why would he be doing good things for people?

BIBLE DISCOVERY

Fill in the blanks:

1. By healing the paralytic, Jesus demonstrated his _____.

2. At a funeral procession, Jesus demonstrated his power over _____.

3. During a storm on a fishing trip, Jesus demonstrated his power over .

4. In his encounter with a man possesessed by demons, Jesus demonstrated his authority over _____.

WHAT DO YOU KNOW?

Do you know anyone else who has authority and power over:

1. Sin and sickness

2. Death

3. The laws of nature

4. The spirit world

Based on these, who do you say that Jesus is? In the next chapter, we'll take a closer look at the possible options.

Is Jesus Really God?
unit three - day four

For nearly three years, Jesus' disciples had followed him, witnessing evidences of his moral and miraculous life. Then Jesus decided it was time for a break. He invited his disciples up north to the area of Mount Hermon for a retreat. It was during this retreat that he asked them, "Who do you say that I am?"[1]

Today–2,000 years later–this question is still the important one. What would you say if he asked you? What are the possible options concerning Jesus? Jesus claimed to be God. Either he is, or he is not who he claimed to be.

Jesus Claimed to be God

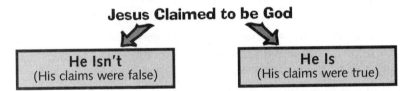

He Isn't (His claims were false)	He Is (His claims were true)

Surveys indicate that about 95 percent of Americans believe there is a God.[2] But when asked if Jesus is this God—and the only God—many aren't so sure. It is common for people to respect Jesus as a prophet or a great moral teacher, but not accept him as the exclusive God of the universe. But is this position logical in light of Jesus' own claim?

If Jesus claimed to be God and he is not, then either he knew it or he didn't know it. If he claimed to be God knowing that he wasn't, he is a LIAR. If he claimed to be God, but didn't know he wasn't, he is a LUNATIC.

Jesus Claimed to be God

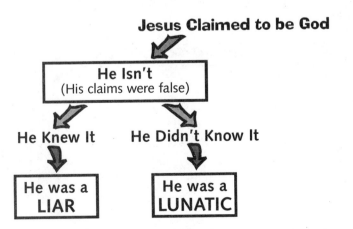

He Isn't
(His claims were false)

He Knew It · He Didn't Know It

He was a LIAR	He was a LUNATIC

Did Jesus lie about being God?

What does "having faith" really mean?

Is religion for gullible people?

How do you know what to believe?

Jesus made some pretty big claims for himself.

When invited to worship the devil in exchange for an earthly kingdom, Jesus quoted the Law: "You shall worship the Lord your God and serve Him only." Later, during his ministry, his followers directed their worship toward him, and he accepted it without protest. I realized that if Jesus knew he wasn't God, I'd have to conclude he was a major hypocrite.

– Dr. Don

DEFINITION:

Psychosis: A severe mental disorder that usually causes erratic and bizarre behavior. Those who have this disorder tend to drive people away. Sometimes they are placed in hospitals and heavily medicated.

A closer look at the options

Option #1

Jesus was a LIAR. He knew that he lied about being God.

If Jesus was a liar, he lied about his own identity. He also received worship as if he were God Almighty. If Jesus knew his claims to be God were false, he would be the greatest liar that ever lived. He'd have deceived more people than anyone else in history.

Yet historical evidence shows that Jesus was a person of virtue and integrity. Many Jewish religious leaders who didn't believe Jesus was God concluded that he was at least a great prophet. People of other religions, including Islam and Eastern faiths, recognize Jesus as a great moral teacher. And when asked, it's not uncommon for people around the world to say they are unsure about Jesus' deity, but are certain that he was a wonderful human being. But if Jesus was the greatest liar that ever lived, how could he also be a wonderful person and a great moral teacher?

> Jesus' executioners said, "He must die, for he made himself out to be the Son of God." Jesus would be a fool if he lied about who he was, and then died for what he knew was a lie.

OPTION #2

Jesus was a LUNATIC. He didn't know that his claims to be God were false.

Were Jesus' claims based on delusions? Sometimes we hear about mentally ill people who make grandiose claims, believing they are real. But these people are quickly diagnosed as **psychotic**.

Jesus attracted large crowds when he preached and had loyal followers throughout his three and one-half years of ministry. The only thing he asked of his followers is that they believe in him. In the end, all but one of Jesus' apostles became martyrs rather than deny that he was their Messiah and Lord.

AN EXPERT OPINION

Could Jesus have been deluded? Not according to practicing psychiatrist Hyder of New York City. He analyzed the records of Jesus' behavior, personality and relationships. He determined Jesus to be a person of excellent mental health. In his book, *Jesus: God, Ghost or Guru?*, he concluded that anyone who says Jesus was deluded, does so "without any psychological evidence in its support" and "in spite of considerable evidence to the contrary."[3]

Contrast the behavior of Jesus to the people we would classify as insane today. Charles Manson is one example. He drugged and persuaded his followers to do all sorts of evil behavior, including murder. His immediate followers, who are in prison for their actions, now realize and admit the sickness of their behavior and of Manson's requests.

Some people who realize that Jesus couldn't have been a liar, and that the evidence doesn't support the view that he was crazy, point to another option—one that is not included in our diagram. They believe that Jesus is a legend. But is this likely?

OPTION # 3
Jesus was a LEGEND.

In the 19th century, it might have been reasonable to suspect Jesus was only a legend. Back then, people believed the New Testament accounts of Jesus were written in the second century—more than 100 years after he lived. By that time, no one was alive who had any firsthand knowledge of what Jesus said or did.

But today, modern discoveries of science have made this view unreasonable. We know from archaeology that the New Testament accounts of Jesus were written within the lifetime of eyewitnesses of Jesus. If the stories about him were not true, the Jews living in Palestine would certainly know it. And they would not have been willing to follow him—or to face the hardships and persecution that came along with doing so.

Writers other than those who wrote the Bible also have testified that Jesus was a real person. Josephus, a Jewish historian, and the Roman historians, Tacitus and Seutonius, all mention Jesus in their writings within 65 to 90 years of his crucifixion.[4]

We know also that real people became believers after claiming to have met or known Jesus. For instance, Saul, a highly educated man and well-known persecutor of Christians, testified that he became a Christian because of a dramatic encounter with the risen Jesus.[5] He then became known as the apostle Paul.

TRANSFORMED

History records show that a man named Saul, who once persecuted Christians, became a Christian after claiming to have an encounter with the risen Jesus. The experience was so profound that he spent the rest of his life traveling to tell others about Jesus. He was eventually martyred for his faith.

ABOUT LEGENDS

Julius Muller, a researcher, has challenged scholars of his day to find even one historical example, in which a fictitious legend about an individual became accepted as true within the lifetime of the eyewitnesses of that person. His challenge has never been met.

DEFINITION

Incarnation: The term used to describe what happened when the eternal Son of God voluntarily became human without diminishing his divine nature. In other words, Jesus was God incarnate. The incarnation made it possible for Jesus to be one person with two united natures.

> "In fact, my mind could not conjure up a single explanation that fit the evidence of history nearly as well as the conclusion that Jesus was who he claimed to be: the one and only Son of God."
>
> —Lee Strobel, former legal editor of Chicago Tribune[6]

Option #4
Jesus is who he claimed to be. He is the LORD.

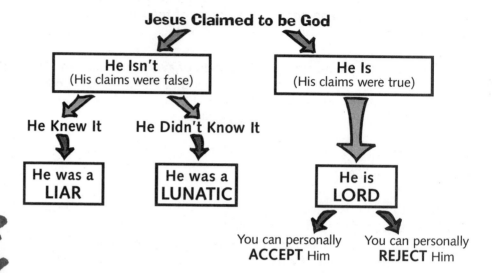

Jesus Claimed to be God

He Isn't (His claims were false) | **He Is** (His claims were true)

He Knew It | **He Didn't Know It**

He was a **LIAR** | He was a **LUNATIC** | He is **LORD**

You can personally **ACCEPT** Him | You can personally **REJECT** Him

If the evidence doesn't support the other three options, there is only one left. The Jesus of history is the incarnate, infinite and personal God who created all things. He is the only person in the universe with two natures—both God and man. Does this seem hard to comprehend? Perhaps one final consideration will help. We'll explore that in the next section.

THINK ABOUT IT

Fill in the blanks based on the information above:

1. Can you think of any other options concerning Jesus other than the four mentioned in this section—a liar, a lunatic, a legend or God? Explain.
   _____.

2. Why doesn't the argument hold up that the stories about Jesus were simply legends?_____.

3. What does the evidence show concerning Jesus?
   _____

The Critical Evidence:
Jesus' Real Resurrection
unit three - day five

For what I received I passed on to you...that Christ died for our sins according to the Scriptures, and that he was buried, that he was raised on the third day according to the Scriptures, and that he appeared to Peter, and then to the Twelve.   1 Corinthians 15:3-5

Jesus promised several times during his ministry that he would rise from the dead. When asked by the Jews what evidence he would give to prove who he was, he responded: "Destroy this temple, and in three days, I will raise it up."[1] He was, in fact, speaking of his own body. His resurrection would be the central test to determine if he was God.

It is interesting to note that people continue to pay their respects at the tombs of other founders of world religions (like Buddha and Muhammad). But Christians don't go to the site of Jesus' tomb thinking he's there. They know he's alive! No other known religious authority has ever risen from the dead.

But what proof do we have of Jesus' resurrection? Even the disciples were skeptical at first. In fact, when a woman came from the grave site to tell them she had seen the resurrected Jesus, they described her report as sheer imagination.[2] What changed their minds?

"Accordingly, if all the evidence is weighed carefully and fairly, it is indeed justifiable, according to the canons of historical research, to conclude that the tomb of Joseph of Arimathea, in which Jesus was buried, was actually empty on the morning of the first Easter. And no shred of evidence has yet been discovered in literary sources, epigraphy, or archaeology that would disprove this statement."[3]

–Dr. Paul Maier, historian at Western Michigan University

The empty tomb

Jewish sources, who were in the best position to know, never denied that Jesus' tomb was empty three days after he died. They only tried to explain why it was empty:

While the women were on their way, some of the guards went into the city and reported to the chief priests everything that had happened. When the chief priest had met with the elders and devised a plan, they gave the soldiers a large sum of money, telling them, "You are to say, 'His disciples came during the night and stole him away while we were asleep.'"   Matthew 28:11-13

A CHANGE OF MIND

Check out James' change of mind and vocation as a result of seeing the resurrected Jesus in John 7:3-5 and 1 Corinthians 15:7, Acts 15:13 and Acts 21:18. Read about Paul's conversion in Acts 22 and 26.

REACTIONS

Read about the disciple's first reaction during his arrest, trial and crucifixion in Mark 14:50, 66-72.

As a fellow juror, I've made my decision. After examining this carefully, I must testify that the evidence supports the God hypothesis. As much as anything from ancient times can be proved, the evidence points to Jesus of Nazareth as the incarnation on this earth of the infinite and personal God. The implications of this truth, once I discovered it, significantly changed my life.
– Dr. Don

People saw Jesus alive

The apostle Paul reports that the resurrected Jesus appeared first to the apostle Peter, then to the entire group of apostles. He says that Jesus later appeared to "more than 500 brethren at one time, most of whom remain until now."[4] Why would Paul make such a point of mentioning that most of the 500 eyewitnesses were still alive, unless he wanted to emphasize that they were available for questioning?

Jesus also made an appearance to James, a half-brother of his who had previously rejected him.[5] This brother was so convinced of Jesus deity after seeing him alive that he later became the head of the Jerusalem Christian church.[6] And Jesus' appearance to Saul of Tarsus, who had been a persecutor of Christians made such an impact on him that he committed his life to serving Jesus. His Christian name became Paul, and he spent the rest of his life telling others about Jesus.[7]

The disciples were radically changed

It is a well-known fact that Jesus' disciples abandoned him and denied even knowing him during his arrest, trial and crucifixion.[8] They were afraid that the Romans might do the same to them too, because of their association with Jesus. But when Jesus appeared alive to the disciples three days after his death, they were transformed. They came out of hiding and began boldly talking about Jesus' resurrection. At least ten of the twelve apostles died a martyr's death—and none ever denied seeing Jesus alive after his death.

Compare the disciples behavior to the behavior of those involved in a modern cover-up—the Watergate affair. The sophisticated lawyers involved in the Watergate affair of the 1970's came clean regarding their fraudulent cover-up when they were faced with the threat of a few years in prison.

What is the verdict?

You have now reviewed the facts of the case. It's up to you to judge the evidence. Is it reasonable to consider Jesus a liar, a lunatic, or only a wonderful moral teacher (rather than God)?

"The crux of the problem of whether Jesus was, or was not, what he proclaimed himself to be must surely depend upon the truth or otherwise of the resurrection. On that greater point we are not merely asked to have faith. In its favor as a living truth there exists such overwhelming evidence, positive and negative, factual and circumstantial, that no intelligent jury in the world could fail to bring in a verdict that the resurrection story is true."[9]
—Lord Darling
(former Chief Justice of England)

I am trying here to prevent anyone saying the really foolish thing that people often say about Him: "I'm ready to accept Jesus as a great moral teacher, but I don't accept His claim to be God." That is the one thing we must not say. A man who was merely a man and said the sort of things Jesus said would not be a great moral teacher. He would either be a lunatic—on a level with a man who says he is a poached egg—or else he would be the Devil of Hell. You must make your choice. Either this man was, and is, the Son of God: or else a madman or something worse. You can shut Him up for a fool, you can spit at Him and kill Him as a demon: or you can fall at His feet and call him Lord and God. But let us not come with any patronizing nonsense about His being a great human teacher. He has not left that open to us. He did not intend to.[10]

—*C. S. Lewis*

Our field trip through the New Testament only covered some of the highlights of Jesus' life. But it gave us an opportunity to examine much of the historical evidence. As a fellow juror, I've made my decision about Jesus, and committed my life to him. Now you have the opportunity to affirm him as your personal Lord as well. You also have the freedom to ignore him or turn away. But is that really what you want to do? Remember, you can't take the matter lightly—the stakes of turning away are too high.

ABOUT LIARS

Gary Habermas, apologetic expert on the resurrection, says, "liars do not make martyrs."

I realized by this point that something very convincing must have happened to the disciples to change their cowardly behavior so dramatically. Their transformation after seeing Jesus showed that they really believed that Jesus rose from the dead. Although claims were made that they somehow arranged for the body to be stolen from the grave, that doesn't make sense. Think about it. Would the disciples all have been willing to die for Jesus if they knew that what they were saying about him was a lie?

– *Dr. Don*

FOR MEMORY

"Because you have seen me, you have believed; blessed are those who have not seen and yet have believed."

John 20:29

BIBLE DISCOVERY

Look up the following verses from Scripture and fill in the blanks (Keep in mind that "Son of Man" was how Jesus often referred to himself):

1. Mark 8:31 - The Son of Man is going to be betrayed into the hands of men. They will kill him, and after three days _____.

2. Mark 9:9 - As they were coming down from the mountain, Jesus gave them orders not to tell anyone what they had seen until the Son of Man

   _____.

3. Mark 9: 31 - He said to them, "The Son of Man is going to be betrayed into the hands of men. They will kill him, and after three days

   _____."

4. Mark 10:33,34 - They will condemn him to death, and will hand him over to the Gentiles, who will mock him and spit on him, flog him and kill him. Three days later _____.

Read John 20:24-28. What did it take to convince Thomas that Jesus was really alive?

_____

_____

Read John 11:25, 26 for yourself what Jesus says, and fill in the blanks:

"I am the _____ and the _____; he who believes in me shall _____ even if he _____, and everyone who lives and _____ in me shall never die."

What now?

After Jesus stated that he was the "Resurrection and the Life," he asked, "Do you believe this?" [11] There are a lot of people who go to church and may have heard the words of Jesus many times. Yet they have never experienced a changed life as a result. Why do you think this is so? We'll explain that next.

Searching for a Reasonable Faith

What Is Faith Really?

unit four - day one

One day I was talking with a young woman who was deeply convicted about committing her life to follow Jesus. Yet, she was hesitant. I'll never forget the reason. It wasn't issues like purpose in life, the reliability of the Bible or the deity of Jesus. Concerning these issues, she was satisfied. Instead, her hesitation was based on fear: "Will it make me into a sap?"

Perhaps you can relate to her, since similar reactions are common: What will God do to me, or expect from me, if I make a faith commitment? Will I turn into a religious geek—be out of touch with reality? What will my friends think?

These feelings often stem from false stereotypes about faith. In other words, most people's fears about faith are based on a misunderstanding of what faith really means.

Misunderstandings and bad examples of faith

People often view faith as ignorance—a distant second or third best way of operating in life. Knowledge is assumed to be the best way. If one cannot know, the next best thing is to believe it anyway. The implication is that faith is uncertain, blind, a crutch for the weak or for those who aren't smart enough to know the difference (a "sap").

Sometimes religious people contribute to misunderstandings. A recent national news story focused on a court case in which parents were being tried for the death of their daughter. What was their alleged crime? They had "faith" that God would heal their daughter. They refused any medical care for her. She died. This was not an appealing picture of faith for those who don't want to become a "sap" for believing in Jesus.

Impressions about faith are often generated by what is seen in other people. Many have been negatively influenced by the much-publicized fiasco of fallen televangelists Jim and Tammy Baker. Or perhaps you have an eccentric neighbor or strange relative who professes faith, and you think, "I don't want to be like that."

FOR MEMORY

Now faith is being sure of what we hope for and certain of what we do not see.

Hebrews 11:1

FALSE DEFINITIONS
Comment by a middle school student: "Faith is believing what you know isn't true."

Comment by a university student: "Faith is believing what you can't know."

AN EXERCISE

Try interchanging the words "faith" and "trust" for "believe" in the following familiar Bible verse from John 3:16:

"For God so loved the world that he gave his one and only Son, that whoever believes [has faith or trusts] in him shall not perish but have eternal life."

Does doing this change the meaning of the verse?

PAUL'S POINT

Faith must have a real object. This is the point made by the apostle Paul in a letter to the Christians at the city of Corinth, "...if Christ has not been raised [from the dead], then our preaching is vain, your faith also is vain. ...your faith is worthless."
1 Corinthian 15:14-17

A tragic story I once heard on the news also illustrates why sincerity is not the same as faith. A nurse at a hospital connected a patient to what was labeled an "oxygen" source. He immediately died. The source had been mislabeled. It was actually a poisonous gas. I think we can assume the nurse was sincere in her belief that the gas was oxygen. But she was sincerely wrong. The object of her faith was defective. Therefore, her faith (trust) was in vain.
– Dr. Don

Going straight to the source

Why can't faith be reasonable? It can according to the Bible! But you won't find reasonable faith by looking at people who set bad examples. Let's go straight to the source of faith to find some insights about it.

Before we get into the Bible, keep in mind that the English words "faith" and "believe" come from the same Greek word. They differ only in that "faith" is the noun and "believe" is the verb form. They really refer to the same thing. A close **synonym** is "trust."

Understanding the real thing

The Bible identifies three parts essential to a genuine faith:

#1: KNOWLEDGE is an essential part of personal faith
Does the university student's statement "faith is believing what you cannot know" seem to make sense to you? Then try substituting the word "trust" for the word "faith." For instance, if I asked, "Do you trust Albert?", and you had never met Albert, you'd probably say, "How can I trust him when I don't even know him?" If you can't *trust* what you do not know, and trust is a synonym for faith, doesn't it make sense that you can't have *faith* in what you do not know either? Substituting the word trust for faith provides a different perspective, doesn't it?

Faith must have a real object

In the New Testament, the apostle Paul gives a definition of faith that is opposite of the university student's. Using logical steps, he explains this to the Christians at Rome.

Sent Ones ➠ Tell ➠ Others Hear ➠ They Believe ➠ They Are Saved

Then Paul draws a conclusion: "Belief, you see, can only come from hearing the message, and the message is the Word of [concerning] Christ."[1] According to this definition, Christian faith can't even get started without knowledge of Jesus. Can you believe (have faith) in Jesus if you have never heard of him? Of course not. That's because we don't believe in "nothing,"we believe in "something." Faith must have an object. That's why we couldn't talk about faith until now—in our search we had to first make certain that Jesus was a genuine and real object that could be trusted.

Does sincerity make faith genuine?

Faith is not the same as positive thinking or sincerity, nor will those qualities make faith genuine. Suppose someone asked if I believed that a certain chair could hold me. If the chair looked normal, and others were sitting in similar chairs, I'd say yes. But what if someone had cut the chair legs almost through, so a slight touch would cause it to collapse? My sincere belief wouldn't do much good then. My faith is only as good as the object in which I place it. If the chair is good, my faith (or trust) in it will be good as well. But if the chair is bad, no matter how sincere I am, I am destined for a fall.

Now we can understand why knowledge is essential to a genuine and real Christian faith. The object of Christian faith is the person of Jesus Christ. If someone had legitimate information to show that Jesus is not the Son of God, then it wouldn't make any difference how sincere or confident Christian believers are. Their sincerity can't make it be true.

We can only have faith in Jesus if we know about him. And our faith is good only if we have a reliable and eyewitness source like the New Testament that demonstrates with reasonable certainty that he is truly God.

#2: WILL is an essential part of personal faith

There's a story told about a stunt man capable of walking a tightwire that was strung across the expanse of Niagara Falls. He had once accomplished the feat while pushing a wheelbarrow. Promoters of the event asked the cheering crowd how many believed the stunt man could do it again. The crowd roared affirmatively. They then asked for a volunteer to ride in the wheelbarrow. No one came forward!

Knowledge is one thing. The crowd said that they knew that the stunt man could do it again. But no one was willing to commit their life to that "faith."

According to Paul, the Israelites had a "will" problem too. He said that not all the Israelites accepted the good news. As Isaiah says, *"Lord, who has believed our message?"...But I ask: Did they not hear? Of course they did.... Again I ask: Did Israel not understand? ...But concerning Israel, he [God] says, "All day long I have held out my hands to a disobedient and obstinate people."* Romans 10:16-21

The people of Israel lacked faith. Why? Was it a lack of knowledge of what God promised? According to Paul, the answer is no. It was due to their disobedience. They had a "will" problem that kept them from believing and obeying God.

I couldn't even get started in the area of personal faith without using my mind to interact with the evidence concerning who Jesus is. And I had evidence from a reliable source—the New Testament.

– Dr. Don

PONDERING THE "WILL" PROBLEM

Provide a few examples from your life when you had a will problem, rather than a knowledge one.

_____
_____
_____

Perhaps you listed some things like disobeying your parents' instructions to be in by midnight, missing the English paper deadline, telling the secret you promised not to tell. In such situations, the problem isn't that you didn't know what was right. You didn't have the will to follow through—you didn't want to do it. Faith is like that. Earlier in our faith search we learned a lot about Jesus. But knowledge doesn't become faith unless we are willing to follow him. A will that says "yes" is the second essential part of the Bible's definition of faith.

One day I asked my two sons to mow the lawn. When I came home later that day, it wasn't done. I asked a familiar "parent" question: "Didn't you hear me?" I really didn't think that at the moment I told them to mow the lawn the physics of sound waves had failed. I was quite sure that my voice had reached their ears, but I was giving them the benefit of the doubt. As it turned out, they did not have a knowledge problem. They had a "will" problem!
— Dr. Don

We have discovered that an essential part of faith is knowing who Jesus is. But it is only one part. Like the Israelites, we can know every detail about Jesus Christ's life, yet have no faith at all. Why?

#3: RESPONSE is an essential part of personal faith

Is it possible to know the truth about Jesus—even be in agreement with it (willing), but still not have genuine faith? Yes it is.

> **Knowing about Jesus ‖ Willingness to follow him ⫮ Genuine faith**

Jesus tells a story that identifies a third essential part of faith:

"What do you think? There was a man who had two sons. He went to the first and said, 'Son, go and work today in the vineyard.' 'I will not,' he answered, but later he changed his mind and went. Then the father went to the other son and said the same thing. He answered, 'I will sir,' but he did not go. Which of the two did what his father wanted?" "The first," they answered. Jesus said to them, "I tell you the truth, the tax collectors and the prostitutes are entering the kingdom of God ahead of you. For John came to you to show you the way of righteousness, and you did not believe him, but the tax collectors and the prostitutes did. And even after you saw this, you did not repent and believe him." Matthew 21:28-32

Jesus' point is that action—or response—is the test of whether a faith commitment is genuine. Without response, we only have good intentions. If our knowledge and our will do not result in a personal response, we will fall short of true faith.

BIBLE DISCOVERY

Look up Romans 10:13-15 and fill in the following blanks:

1. Everyone who calls on the name of the Lord will be _____.

2. But how can they call on one they have not _____?

3. And how can they believe in that one if they have not _____ of him?

4. And how can they hear of him without someone _____ them?

5. And how can they tell about him unless they are _____?

Traveling the Faith Triangle

unit four - day two

If we use the three corners of a triangle to represent the three essential parts of personal faith, we can define faith in a dynamic way: Faith is traveling the triangle.

Jesus talked about two kinds of people: those who travel the faith triangle and those who don't. The consequences in their lives are amazingly different as you find in the Bible Discovery below.

I sometimes hear people say they wish they had someone else's faith—Mother Teresa's or their grandpa's or Billy Graham's. Yet I often discover that they have just the amount of faith they are willing to have. Even though they have the knowledge of Jesus, they have not acted on it. They have not responded by committing their life to follow Jesus.

Genuine personal faith has the power to start us down the path to becoming like Jesus—to impact everything about our lives in a positive way. But religion can't and won't. Believing that God exists won't either. Do you have the real thing? As we continue our faith search I'll show you how you can know and the powerful difference it can make in your life.

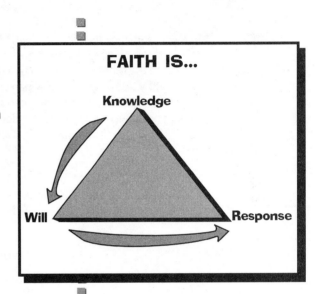

FAITH IS...

Knowledge

Will

Response

 BIBLE DISCOVERY

Read Matthew 7:21- 27 and fill in the blanks:

1. How does Jesus describe those who come to him and hear his words and act upon them? _____

2. What does Jesus say will happen to people who hear and act on his words?

    _____

3. How does Jesus describe those who hear his words and do not act accordingly?

    _____

4. What does he say will happen to those who don't act after hearing his words?

    _____

The fish story below isn't about a positive situation. But it does illustrate involvement—and true faith requires involvement. So what kind of involvement does faith require? Perhaps the following two illustrations will help to explain faith involvement.

A FISH STORY

The story is told of a fisherman who was famous for his track record of catching fish. But he always fished alone, so no one knew how he did it. An elderly man begged the fisherman to teach him the sport as a retirement hobby. Although the fisherman was reluctant to give away his secret, the older man's persistence finally won out. Once on the lake, the elderly man was surprised that the great fisherman had only a metal box and a net for fishing gear.

As they came to a remote corner of the lake, the fisherman left the boat motor running, opened his metal box and pulled out some dynamite sticks. He lit them, heaved them overboard, then put the motor in full gear to speed out of the way. After the blast was over, he circled back to net the fish that had been stunned by the explosion. By then the older man had seen enough. He pulled his game warden badge from his pocket and flashed it before the fisherman. The fisherman paused a moment, then pulled out more dynamite, lit it and shoved it into the game warden's hand saying, "Now are you going to fish—or are you just going to sit there?"[1]

#1 Faith is a "head to foot commitment"

As a biology teacher, I tend to assume that biology is everyone's favorite school subject. Whether or not you agree, I think you'll relate to my simple anatomy comparison to faith. Let's bring back the faith triangle introduced earlier and compare each point of the triangle to an appropriate body part.

I rejected the "head, heart and feet" definition of faith when I was a skeptic because I couldn't imagine faith starting with the head— including evidence and reason. I thought that people of faith checked their brains at the door of the church. Yet this definition says that the mind can be satisfied.
– Dr. Don

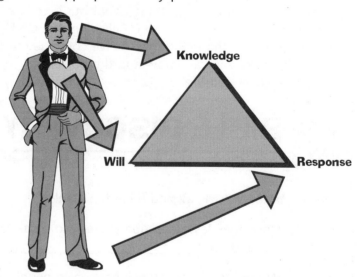

From this triangle illustration, we can get a simple definition: **Faith is making a commitment to God from head to foot.** It starts with the head (with knowledge and reason). From there the process figuratively moves to the heart. Here the will must interact with the information learned concerning Jesus. If my will is persuaded and convicted that Jesus is legitimate, the faith process moves to the feet—the place where there is to be a life response. When the response is made, the whole person is satisfied and a personal faith relationship with Jesus begins.

#2 Faith is a "commitment-making process"

I also like to define faith as a commitment-making process. To illustrate this, consider the steps involved in starting a new business—say a fast-food restaurant. I'd most likely start by doing some market research. I'd find out what the people in the area enjoyed eating and how many competing businesses were around. I'd explore possible building sites, research costs and check out other details of constructing a restaurant. Gathering this kind of important information is equivalent to the "knowledge" part of faith.

But just because I've gathered a lot of information doesn't mean I have a restaurant. The information only serves to help me decide whether or not to build. Even if the commitment to build is made, I still do not have a business. I must take action—construct the building, contact suppliers, and hire staff to run the restaurant. Only when the first hamburger that comes off the grill is paid for can I claim to have a fast-food restaurant.

The steps in the commitment-making process just described are like those involved in traveling the faith triangle. First, I become familiar with the person of Jesus Christ. Then I am convicted that he is my Savior, the Son of God. Finally, I respond to that conviction by following him in obedience.

At one point in my life I realized that I didn't have the real thing. How about you? Do you have the real thing? In the next section of our faith search I'll show you how you can know whether you do—and the powerful difference it can make in your life.

– Dr. Don

Two Conditions
of the Faith Commitment
unit four - day three

Now that we're familiar with the essential components of faith and the nature of commitment, we can talk about the conditions of the faith commitment.

Condition #1
It is to be based on the Word of God
The first condition is that the source of the information (knowledge) is the Word of God. That includes the evidence about the Bible and Jesus Christ that we have already shown is reliable. We also see evidences for God through the natural world—like beauty, order and design.

Condition #2
It is to be without regard to the emotional questioning of that Word
The second condition acknowledges the reality of our human emotions, but requires that these emotions not determine the outcome of the commitment-making process of faith.

Emotions can add depth to your experience, but should not be considered a priority in the commitment-making process. If you allow that to happen, emotions such as pride or insecurity (a desire to be popular) might prevent you from making a commitment to follow Christ.

Abraham's faith commitment

The Old Testament patriarch, Abraham, provides a perfect example of faith as a commitment-making process that transcends emotions. Perhaps you've heard the Genesis story of how God had promised to give Abraham and his wife Sarah a son. Through that son, he promised them descendants "as the stars of the heavens," and that through one of their son's descendants "all the nations of the earth shall be blessed."[1] That son, whom Abraham and Sarah named Isaac, didn't arrive until they were very old, and as you can imagine, he was special and dear to them—a "miracle" baby.

When Isaac had grown to be a young boy, God came to Abraham and tested his faith: "Take now your son, your only son, whom you love, Isaac, and go to the land of Moriah; and offer him there as a burnt offering on one of the mountains of which I will tell you."[2]

A QUICK REVIEW

The three essential components of faith are

1._____

2._____

3._____

Faith is a _____ making process.

EMOTIONS
Human emotions are not always a guide for what is right. For example, jealousy, lust, depression and insecurity are examples of real human emotions. But when we take action based on these emotions, it is often a big mistake.

Religion or just believing in God won't get us very far. Only genuine personal faith has the power to start us on the path to becoming like Jesus.

ABOUT SACRIFICE

Although the idea of sacrificing a person is repulsive, it was not an uncommon practice among the other people living in Palestine at the time of Abraham. Furthermore, this event was a picture image of what God did 2,000 years later when he sacrificed his only son for us.

JESUS' SACRIFICE

Christians recognize the fact that God sacrificed his only son so that we may be saved as the single most important event in the history of mankind.

One could have thought of a lot of excuses for sleeping in late the next morning after hearing a message like that. But not Abraham—he arose early. He chose (by his will) to be obedient (respond) to the word from God that he had received (knowledge). The emotional questioning that undoubtedly flooded through him did not determine his response.

However, he did struggle. How could God fulfill the promises that he made concerning Isaac if Isaac was dead? Yet he knew God as the One who is totally righteous—that God could not lie or be unfaithful to his promises. By the time Abraham arrived at the place of sacrifice three days later, he had resolved it in his mind: Abraham reasoned that God could raise the dead.[3]

As Abraham prepared to complete his agonizing task, Isaac (who was accustomed to lambs being sacrificed) asked, "Where is the lamb for the burnt offering?" Abraham must have gulped, but managed to say, "God himself will provide the lamb for the burnt offering, my son." But not until Abraham reached for his knife to slay his son did God cry out, "Do not lay a hand on the boy.... Now I know that you fear God, because you have not withheld from me your son, your only son." With great rejoicing, Abraham followed God's instruction to retrieve a ram caught by his horns in some nearby bushes, and offer that ram as a substitute for his son. God did provide the lamb for Abraham and Isaac! Abraham was so grateful that he called God *Jehovah-Jireh*, which in Hebrew means "The Lord Who Provides."

A DEEPER MEANING

This dramatic story of Abraham and his son has even deeper meaning. It took place about 1900 BC in the land of Moriah, the same place where the city of Jerusalem was later built. After Abraham's time, one particular mountain became known as Mount Moriah. In Hebrew this means "The Place of Provision." The Jews later constructed their temple on this same hill. Amazingly, this is also where John the Baptist introduced Jesus as "the Lamb of God who takes away the sin of the world." The ram that was sent to spare Abraham's son physically on Mount Moriah foretold of the spiritual Lamb that would come 2,000 years later to the same mount to die on the cross so that we may have spiritual and eternal life. Jesus is that spiritual Lamb. The Bible tells us that all who have the same faith as Abraham are his true children.

If we trust Jesus Christ as our Savior and Lord, then we are among the "stars of the heavens"—we are the spiritual descendants that God promised Abraham about 4,000 years ago. *"Therefore, be sure that it is those who are of faith that are sons of Abraham."*

Galations 3:7

Can Faith
Really Change My Life?
unit four - day four

Knowing the three essential parts of faith and understanding definitions of faith don't automatically lead to a personal response. A Christian is one who embraces Jesus Christ and thus receives life-changing gifts from God—a new relationship, a new freedom and a new hope. Let's look closer at the gifts that are provided to those who make a personal response to God.

A NEW RELATIONSHIP

Faith is not choosing a set of spiritual guidelines to follow. Faith is a relationship with God. Here is how Jesus expressed it: "If anyone is thirsty, let him come to me and drink. Whoever believes in me, as the scripture has said, streams of living water will flow from within him."[1] He spoke of the Spirit which those who believed in him were to receive.

God's PRESENCE

Jesus is referring to a supernatural gift—the Holy Spirit. Perhaps this idea of God living in you seems hard to comprehend. Take time right now to verify this truth by doing the Bible Discovery below.

I recall fearing that being a Christian would require following an impossible set of rules. It also seemed that there were a lot of hypocrites in the Christian church, and I didn't want to be one of them. At that time, I didn't really understand how to become a Christian and didn't know about the gifts that God provides for those who follow Jesus Christ.

– Dr. Don

BIBLE DISCOVERY

Look up John 14:16-17.
What did Jesus promise to his disciples?_____
Where will this gift reside?_____

The apostle Paul also affirms that God lives in Christians. Read how he explained this to the earliest Christians in I Corinthians 6:19 and fill in the blanks:

"Or do you not know that your body is a _____ of the _____ who is in you, whom you have from _____, and that you are not your own?"

How do we become a temple of the Holy Spirit? Paul explains in his letter to Christian believers in the city of Ephesus. Read Ephesians 1:13,14 and answer the following questions.

What response do we need to have to be saved, i.e., included in Christ?_____
How are we "marked" or identified as a Christian?_____
What does that guarantee?_____

I grew up thinking that no one in this life could ever know whether or not they were going to heaven. After all, only God would know how my good and bad thoughts and deeds added up. My part was to try as hard as I could and hope I did better than a lot of other people. Then, if God graded on a curve, I'd likely make it. But this belief is not from the Bible. If my relationship with God is the result of forgiveness and grace, then my deeds can't be the basis for whether I'll "go to heaven."
– Dr. Don

The Holy Spirit is described by Paul as a "seal"—a mark of authenticity or an assurance that you really are a member of the family of God.[3] The "deposit" is a guarantee that God will never abandon you in this life and assures fulfillment of God's promise for eternal life after death.

You can find disciples of Muhammad or Gandhi, but only in the sense that they try to live by the teachings of these leaders. Since Muhammad and Gandhi are dead, their followers can't have a personal relationship with them. True disciples of Jesus, on the other hand, go beyond modeling their lives by his teachings. A Christian's faith is a relationship with the person of Jesus Christ because he is very much alive, and we will someday see him face to face.

A NEW FREEDOM

We have identified that Christian faith is not so much a religion as it is a relationship with Jesus Christ who is alive. We must also realize that the Christian faith is more than a moral code or ethical system to follow.

Jesus was very direct when he spoke to Nicodemus, a Pharisee. He told Nicodemus that he must have new life from above.[4] By this he meant that the Holy Spirit must conceive new spiritual life within him. Nicodemus could not get to heaven based on following rules or being "good enough."

BIBLE DISCOVERY

Read John 3:1-5 and answer the following questions:

What does Jesus give as a condition for seeing the kingdom of God (going to heaven)?

_____

In verse 5, Jesus says that being born again (receiving new life) involves being born of _____ and of the _____.

According to Jesus, no one can get to heaven by doing good deeds. We become Christians when God does a miracle of new spiritual life within us as we respond in faith to Jesus Christ. The result is a faith in which we experience the gift of the Holy Spirit. This presence of God is the power needed to change us gradually from within to be like Christ. This insight helps to clear the misunderstanding that we can be "good" in and of ourselves. We can try to live up to Jesus' teachings—to love our enemies, avoid lust, give up possessions, forgive others—but we'll always fall short.

This insight helps to clear the misunderstandings that I can be "good" in and of myself. I can try to live up to Jesus' teachings—to love my enemies, avoid lust, give up my possessions, forgive others—but I will always fall short. As Bertrand Russell, the British mathematician and philosopher said: "love your enemies is good advice, but too difficult for us."

Why do we need the gift of God's grace?

Trying to live like Jesus is not just difficult—it's impossible. Most of us try, but we can't. We are morally inadequate to be holy like God. That's why we need the gift of God's grace. The Bible Discovery affirms this teaching. Complete it now.

When we look at these life-changing dimensions of faith, we see that the triangle illustration (with its three essential parts) is still not an adequate representation of faith. The Holy Spirit must be placed as a fourth point at the center to create a supernatural dimension.

The Holy Spirit's role is to convict us to be open—to be persuaded by the evidence concerning Jesus. When we personally respond to the gift of salvation through a faith commitment to Jesus Christ, the Holy Spirit comes to live within us. He also provides the power for us to follow through on that faith response—and gradually transforms us from within to become more like Jesus Christ.

TRINITY
The Holy Spirit is the third person of the Godhead. Jesus Christ and God the Father are the other two persons. God the Father, Jesus the Son and the Holy Spirit together are often referred to as the Holy Trinity.

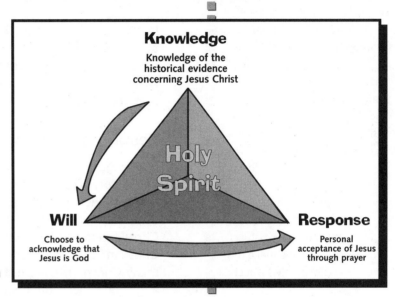

Knowledge
Knowledge of the historical evidence concerning Jesus Christ

Holy Spirit

Will
Choose to acknowledge that Jesus is God

Response
Personal acceptance of Jesus through prayer

BIBLE DISCOVERY

Read the apostle Paul's explanation of the concept of grace in Ephesians 2:8,9 and John 6:65 and fill in the following blanks:

"For it is by _____ you have been saved, through _____ and this not from yourselves, it is the _____ of God—not by works, so that no one can boast.   Ephesians 2:8-9

If you have an interest in God and are convicted to follow him, it's not your own doing. Jesus said that "...no one can _____, unless it has been granted him from the Father." God is at work in your life drawing you to himself.

John 6:65

KEY TESTS

Two questions (or tests) can be used to test the reality of a subjective experience:

1) What is the objective reality that has resulted in the subjective experience?

2) How many other people have had the same subjective experience from being related to this objective reality?

A NEW HOPE

The Christian faith promises a new relationship with the living God. It also promises a new freedom from the treadmill of moral performance—of trying continually to earn his approval. God's grace means forgiveness, and new power and joy.

But that's not all. There is something else new. One of the most familiar sayings of Jesus in the Bible is John 3:16. Read John 3:16 and write it out here:_____

_____

In another of his letters, John says: *"God has given us eternal life, and this life is in his Son. He who has the Son has life; he who does not have the Son of God does not have life. I write these things to you who believe in the name of the Son of God so that you may know that you have eternal life."*   1 John 5:11-13

Testing subjective claims

In previous units we reviewed objective evidence and facts of science and history to show there really is a God, that Jesus is God incarnate, and that the Christian faith is true. In addition to the objective evidence, there is powerful subjective evidence for truth of the Christian faith. It is revealed in experiential changes in the lives of Christians that demonstrate the reality of their faith. For example, many Christians have testified that faith in Jesus has freed them from addictions, given them victory over anger or provided a reason to live. However, some people argue that these Christian testimonies don't really prove anything—they are just based on imagination or emotion. So, how can we know? Take time to read "A Tomato in a Shoe" and the two "Key Tests" in the margin.

As a Christian, when I'm asked what objective reality represents my changed life, I answer, "Faith in the person of Jesus Christ and His gift of the Holy Spirit in me." There are millions of people from every nationality and profession who claim to have this same positive life change as the result of a relationship with Jesus Christ. When millions of people are giving similar testimonies, it reinforces the objective reality—Jesus can change lives!

"Who do you say that I am?"
Before Jesus left this earth he told his followers that he was going to prepare a place for them in heaven and would come back to get them.

"And if I go and prepare a place for you, I will come back and take you to be with me that you also may be where I am."   John 14:3

According to the Bible, the time is also coming when every person who has ever lived will stand before Jesus. He will ask them this question: "Who do you say that I am?"[6] How will you answer him?

What Keeps
People from Real Faith?
unit four - day five

Is unbelief always the result of choice?
How does free will fit in?

We've introduced the two components that are essential to faith as a Christian. Again, they are:

1. **Knowing about Jesus, and**

2. **A willingness to respond with a "yes" to him**

Now it's easy to see what prevents a person from becoming a Christian. The reasons are just the opposite of the two components essential to faith.

1. **Ignorance**

2. **Willful rejection**

In other words, people don't have faith in Jesus either because they haven't learned about him, or because they reject and ignore what they have learned about him as being untrue or irrelevant. Let's take a closer look at these two kinds of unbelief.

Unbelief resulting from ignorance

We've discussed negative stereotypes about faith in earlier sections. Sometimes people get so turned off by these stereotypes, they decide just to close their ears to the real evidence. These people are not ignorant due to a lack of available information. They might have even heard it. But they have simply decided not to listen to it or to be open to it. A great illustration of this is presented in the story about a man and his dog on the next page.

The apostle Paul provides another example of a person who acted out of ignorance when it came to faith in Jesus. Before becoming a Christian, he hated Christians so much that he brutally persecuted them. However, once he met Jesus and learned the truth, he admits that he had been acting out of ignorance: "...I was shown mercy because I acted ignorantly in unbelief."[1]

READ ACTS 9:1-6

Here the Bible records the apostle Paul's encounter with Jesus on the road to Damascus. At the time, Paul was heading to Damascus to persecute Christians. Note that in the New Testament times, Christians referred to themselves as followers of the "Way."

> "I do believe; help
> me overcome
> my unbelief!"
>
> Mark 9:24

Unbelief resulting from doubt

Perhaps you feel that you don't have faith, but you know the problem is not a lack of information. It's just that you are questioning—uncertain about it. Is that unbelief? Where does spiritual doubt fit into the subject of faith?

I have asked many people to tell me what comes to their mind when they hear the word "unbelief." To my amazement, I get a wide variety of one-word descriptions:

Doubt · Blind · Rejection · Unsure · Wavering · Distrust · Decision · Rebellion · Ignorance · Indecision · Arrogant · Skepticism · Hard-hearted · Unknowing

---

A MAN, A DOG AND A STEREOTYPE

A man that my wife and I met several years ago is an example of a person with a negative stereotype. Vernee and I were conducting a door-to-door survey to learn people's views about Christian faith. At one home, a burly man answered the door. When I asked if he'd be willing to answer some questions concerning his faith, he exploded into such an angry tirade that his face reddened and his eyes bulged. Fortunately, I managed to hide behind my wife Vernee through most of it!

Finally, the man started to calm down a bit. We changed the subject by complimenting him on his beautiful flower beds and managed to strike up a pleasant conversation on a new subject. By the time we were ready to leave, he was calmer, and I was bold enough to ask why he'd been so upset by our initial question. He confided that at one time his sole companion had been a special pet dog. One day, he had let the dog outside and watched from the window as it wandered over to a "religious" neighbor's shrubbery and did what dogs often do to shrubbery. He said that the neighbor stepped out of the bushes and kicked the dog so hard it nearly flew into the street. To his sorrow, the dog had to be put to sleep. As the man recounted the incident, his face once again turned red and he blurted; "Now if that's what faith is like, I don't want any part of it!"

— *Dr. Don*

Think about the above words and their meanings. It's obvious that even though the words all refer to unbelief, they have very different meanings. For instance, there is quite a difference between "ignorance" and "rejection" or between "wavering" and "rebellion." Are the people who came up with these words confused? Or does the diversity really show that unbelief is a very complex issue?

The three "faces" of unbelief

Let's explore unbelief a bit more. Imagine that a lost tribe has been discovered in the Amazon jungles. As a result of years of isolation, they have never heard of any events concerning human civilization. Therefore, they have no knowledge about Jesus. At this point, they lack faith in Jesus (are in unbelief) for a special reason—ignorance. How can they believe in what they have never heard? These people represent the first "face" of unbelief: IGNORANT UNBELIEF.

But let's say I volunteer to live with these people, learn their language and spend months telling them the historical facts about Jesus Christ. As I share, tribe members have the opportunity to question and debate. Some are persuaded about a point or two, but unsure about others. They go back and forth, but don't arrive at a conclusion about Jesus. They remain in unbelief, but for a different reason—they can't or won't decide. The second necessary part of faith is the will to say "yes"—to make a choice about Jesus. These people now represent the second "face" of unbelief: DOUBT.

However, after further teaching and answering questions, the chief of the tribe stands up to announce the tribe's decision. To my horror, I discover they are a cannibal tribe. Worse yet, the chief says I'm "out to lunch." They reject the message they've heard concerning Jesus. They are still in unbelief, but this time it's because they have chosen not to believe. We've just described people who represent the third "face" of unbelief: DECISIONED UNBELIEF.

The three different "faces" of unbelief through which the lost tribe progressed helps explain why so many different responses come to mind when people are asked to describe unbelief.

Christian faith requires knowing the object of faith— Jesus Christ

"How can they know if they haven't heard."

Romans 10:14,17

To my horror, I discover they are a cannibal tribe. Worse yet the chief says I'm "out to lunch."

 # BIBLE DISCOVERY

From the list of words that people have used to describe unbelief, decide which words best match the various types of unbelief:

Doubt	Unsure	Blind	Rejection	Unknowing	Decision
Wavering	Rebellion	Distrust	Ignorance	Indecision	Arrogant
Skepticism	Hard-hearted				

IGNORANT UNBELIEF _____

DOUBT UNBELIEF _____

DECISIONED UNBELIEF _____

Discovering Real Faith

Getting Out of Unbelief

unit five - day one

Are any of the forms of unbelief we discussed familiar to you? If so, no matter which stage of unbelief you're in, there is a way out. Before I explain further, study the following diagram to see how the three forms of unbelief are related. Knowing how they are related will help you see how it is possible to progress through the various stages of unbelief to faith.

Ignorant Unbelief  **Doubt Unbelief**  **Decisioned Unbelief**

FOR MEMORY

Immediately the boy's father exclaimed, "I do believe; help me overcome my unbelief!"

Mark 9:24

How do I escape ignorant unbelief?

If you are in ignorant unbelief, how do you get out of it? This is a "knowledge" problem. If you've come this far in this study, you may already have resolved it. But many have not. Someone needs to tell them about—and they need to receive—the truths we have already discussed concerning the object of faith, Jesus Christ.

The Aucas' change of heart

Five Christian missionary couples had traveled to South America to tell the Auca Indian tribe about Jesus. The tribe was clearly in ignorant unbelief since no one had ever learned the language to tell them about Jesus. One day, during an attempt to make personal contact with them, all five husbands were killed by the Aucas in a surprise attack. In spite of tremendous grief over the loss of their husbands, the five wives flew over the tribe and dropped gifts from their small airplane. Their act of courage, love and forgiveness won them the chance to interact with the Aucas. Ignorance concerning Jesus was replaced by facts as they taught about Jesus' life and teachings. Many of the Aucas eventually made the commitment to embrace Jesus as their Savior. Incredible changes took place in their hearts. In fact, the chief of the tribe later baptized the son of the missionary he had killed.[1]

Escaping doubt-based unbelief

But what if you are in the condition of unbelief based on doubt concerning Jesus? What is needed to move from that position? This is a problem of "indecision." You must decide how much information is enough to assure you about Jesus' identity, and to say either "yes" or "no" to him as Savior and Lord.

I recall the time in my own life when I could no longer say that I didn't know enough about Jesus—that I was ignorant of the facts. Interestingly, in my own mind, I had not decided to reject him either. Or had I? My first exposure to the evidences for the Bible and faith had left me unsure and wavering—in doubt. But additional months of fact-gathering did not change my indecision. I had already been persuaded that the evidence for Jesus' deity was excellent. Yet I remained in doubt and kept thinking that I needed to read one more book and check out one more fact. Looking back on this time from my perspective today, I believe my skepticism had become, in reality, decisioned unbelief masquerading as doubt.
– Dr. Don

Escaping decisioned unbelief

Finally, what do you need to do if you are in decisioned unbelief? This is a "will" problem. The only way out is to reconsider this position by returning to "doubt" and taking another look at the evidence to see if a "yes" to Jesus is not more reasonable and appropriate than a "no."

Where are you?

The simplicity of knowing the position we are in with regard to Jesus should now be apparent. In the margin I describe my own discovery. What about you? If you have not made a faith commitment to Jesus, which of the three faces of unbelief best fits you? Think carefully about this. What appears on the surface may not always be the real problem.

Remember the story about the man who was so upset about the way his "religious" neighbor treated his dog that the mere mention of faith caused him to burst into rage? Which kind of unbelief do you think he had? To be honest, my first impression was decisioned unbelief because his anger made him appear hard-hearted and rebellious. But after hearing his story, I changed my mind. I think he was in ignorant unbelief. He was rejecting a religious neighbor who had acted foolishly. His anger about that experience made him unwilling to listen to the facts about the genuine Jesus.

THINK ABOUT IT

Like this man, many people remain in ignorant unbelief because they simply can't get past the negative behaviors they have observed in some people who profess to be Christians. I think it is the most common form of unbelief today.

Pause right now and consider where you stand. Be honest. Do you feel that you remain in unbelief for any of the reasons discussed? Write some of your thoughts here.

If you conclude that one of the unbelief positions fit you pretty well, but wish it didn't, the next section contains really good news for you. If you already believe, there will be some valuable insights for you as well.

Describe your position on faith before reading this book. Has it changed? (If so, how?)

_____

_____

_____

_____

Where Am I?
Taking a Stand

unit five - day two

The good news!

The fact that we have free will means we can say "no" to Jesus Christ—reject the Christian faith. But to be truly free means that we can also choose to say "yes" to Jesus and to faith. This is the good news. There is a real alternative to unbelief: faith!

In our faith search, we have had the opportunity to examine key evidence for Jesus. We have now come to a pivotal point. Will you choose Jesus (faith) or reject him (unbelief)?

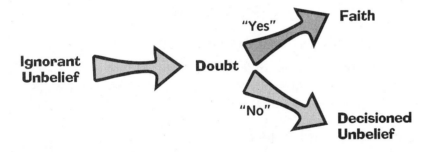

Ignorant Unbelief → **Doubt**
"Yes" → **Faith**
"No" → **Decisioned Unbelief**

Watch out for the counterfeit

We must be careful not to be fooled by a counterfeit faith that masquerades as real faith. When counterfeit faith is mistaken for genuine faith, it invariably leads to disappointment or bitterness (or both) rather than fulfillment and joy.

Counterfeit faith often comes in the form of an unwritten contract with God. It is based on how well God responds to specific personal requests for things like physical comfort, recognition, popularity and success.

> What does it mean to have unconditional faith?
>
> Can faith ever lead to disappointment?
>
> Have I affirmed my faith in Jesus Christ for personal salvation?

The idea that faith requires a personal commitment became clear to me during my own faith search. But what I didn't understand was how faith was to operate in my life. I didn't realize that a counterfeit faith could masquerade as the real thing...I grew up thinking of faith in terms of a contract. In return for my believing in God, he would provide certain benefits for me: happiness, friends, success and wealth —small things! This seemed only right in view of the sacrifice it was for me to conform my life to follow Jesus. And I would continue to follow God as long as he lived up to his end of my imaginary contract—a contract that read, "I'll believe if ..."
— Dr. Don

THINK ABOUT IT

Take a few moments to reflect. Have you put conditions on your faith in God, either in the past or very recently? Have you told God you'll have faith **IF** he answers certain prayers—gives you specific things? Jot down some of your personal thoughts.

_____

_____

_____

_____

Just as the Israelites understood the facts about God but chose a conditional faith, so do some people today.

Bible examples of counterfeit faith

The people of the nation of Israel often tested God with an "I'll believe if..." kind of faith. Through these Bible accounts, we learn about the pitfalls of contract faith.

The Old Testament tells how God rescued the Israelites from slavery under the Egyptians. He paved the way for their escape by performing many miracles, then promised he would lead them safely into the land of Canaan. In spite of all that God did for them, the Israelites often grumbled and turned away from God. For instance, even though food miraculously appeared on the ground each morning during their trek through the desert, they complained because they didn't have more variety or seasonings.[1] More than once, they turned their backs on God and began to worship idols. These people were not in ignorant unbelief! God had clearly revealed himself to them. Just as the Israelites understood the facts about God, but chose a conditional faith, so do some people today. Conditional (contract) faith easily wanes during life's difficulties.

The way the Israelites responded to reports about Canaan also demonstrates their contract faith. Twelve men were sent to spy out the land of Canaan. They returned with conflicting recommendations. Two of the men, Joshua and Caleb, believed God's promise unconditionally. They recommended taking the land. However, the other 10 reported that the inhabitants were like giants and the cities well fortified.[2] There was no way the land could be taken. What would change their minds? Perhaps if they were a super power with stealth bombers and missiles. Their position was, "God, we believe you could take us in, if...." Sadly, this is not faith at all. It is a counterfeit.

Even though God had already promised them the land, the people of Israel followed the majority report. They even wished they could return to slavery in Egypt. Their counterfeit faith led to disappointment and unnecessary suffering for that entire generation of Israelites. God was so angry that he allowed them to wander in the wilderness for 40 years. However, because of his real faith, Joshua eventually was used by God to lead a new generation of Israelites into the promised land.[3]

FOR MEMORY

How long will these people treat me with contempt? How long will they refuse to believe in me, in spite of all the miraculous signs I have performed among them?

Numbers 14:11

Contract faith, the counterfeit, is asking God to perform to our bidding. This is hardly the appropriate attitude of a "finite" toward the "infinite!" We must come to God on God's terms, not on ours.

THINK ABOUT IT

1. Based on Don's testimony and examples from the Old Testament, define contract or counterfeit faith in your own words:

   _____

   _____

2. Reflect on the statement in the margin of this page. How do you feel about that? Write some of your thoughts.

   _____

   _____

Welcome to Genuine Faith

unit five - day three

Genuine faith is not a forced emotion or a confidence placed in circumstances or the church. It is unconditional trust in the infinitely powerful, wise, loving and just God—the God who created and sustains all that exists. What he says he can and does do. Because that is true, the "commitment-making process based on the Word of God" definition of faith is a very reasonable way to live our lives. While counterfeit faith says, "I'll belief if ...", genuine faith simply says, "I believe."

Biblical examples of genuine faith

> "I say to you, not even in Israel have I found such great faith."
>
> **Jesus in Luke 7:9**

THE CENTURION'S GENUINE FAITH: A **centurion** of Jesus' time demonstrated real faith. Jesus commended him, "I say to you, not even in Israel have I found such great faith." What was there about the Centurion's faith that gained such high praise from Jesus?

The man was a military officer who respected and understood authority. He had a favorite servant who was very sick and about to die. As far as we know, this man had never seen Jesus perform a miracle, but had likely heard reports about them. Therefore, he sent some Jewish friends to get Jesus. As Jesus approached his home, the Centurion sent a message, "Lord, don't trouble yourself, for I do not deserve to have you come under my roof. That is why I did not even consider myself worthy to come to you. But say the word, and my servant will be healed."[1]

The Centurion reasoned:

1. Jesus is God
2. God has authority over disease and the power to heal.
3. Therefore, Jesus only needs to speak the command.

The Centurion's humility and confidence sprang from his certainty that Jesus was God. And if he was God, he had authority over disease and the power to heal. The Centurion didn't interject any conditions. He knew that all Jesus had to do was issue the command. He was right. When Jesus spoke, the servant was healed and restored to good health, a fulfilling and joyful result.

REAL FAITH
Real faith is a "commitment-making process based on the word of God." This definition makes sense because what God says, he can and does do.

DEFINITION
Centurion: The term used for a commander of 100 Roman soldiers in Jesus' time.

We can only imagine the scenario when God asked Noah to build the ark. What kind of boat should it be? God said to make it 450 feet long (that's 1½ football fields!), 75 feet wide and 45 feet high with three decks. Not exactly what you complete in a few spare weekends—this project took Noah more than 100 years!

I wonder how Noah handled being a public spectacle in the community. This was not a canoe. He couldn't hide it. And it was hundreds of miles to the nearest large body of water. If you were Noah's son or daughter, do you think you would have been embarrassed? Would you have questioned: "Dad, are you sure you heard that message right?"
– Dr. Don

NOAH'S GENUINE FAITH: The Old Testament tells of a time when the world had become so wicked that God grieved that he had made humans. But one man knew and served God faithfully, and "found favor in the eyes of the Lord."[2] Noah would be spared God's judgment by riding out the coming flood in an ark—that is, if he had faith to follow God's instructions to build it. Keep in mind that when God asked Noah to build the ark, he didn't live on the seaboard. He didn't even have a lakeside cabin! What must Noah have gone through (see the margin)?

> By faith, Noah, being warned by God about things not yet seen, in reverence prepared an ark for the salvation of his household...and became an heir of the righteousness which is according to faith.
>
> **Hebrews 11:7**

The point is that Noah's decision to build the ark was made solely on his belief in God and the authority of his Word. "Thus Noah did; according to all that God had commanded him, so he did."[3] For more than 100 years, he was probably made the brunt of every joke for miles around. But Noah believed God.

By the time the ark was complete, it had begun to rain. Water began to appear where it had never been before. The fool, Noah, began to look like a genius. His formula was really quite simple: He believed God unconditionally. He had genuine faith.

THINK ABOUT IT

1. Define genuine faith in your own words:_____
_____
_____

2. Provide a modern example of genuine faith demonstrated by you or someone you know. If you can't think of any real examples, describe an imaginary scenario.)
_____
_____
_____

Where Are You?

unit five - day four

Now that you've studied the forms of unbelief and understand the difference between genuine and counterfeit faith, what position have you taken—or will you take—in regard to Jesus Christ?

Have I made a faith commitment to Jesus Christ?

Your response to this question alone determines whether you are a "yes" (faith) or a "no" (unbelief) on this diagram. In the faith triangle, we identified three possible reasons for a "no" response.

1. Lack of knowledge
I don't know what Jesus said and did. Why should I have faith in him?

2. Indecision
I still have questions and uncertainty about what I should do.

3. Willful Rejection
I don't believe that Jesus needed to die for me. I don't want to make a commitment to live for him.

During my own search I thought that maybe faith was a personal thing— what works for some may not be for everyone. That was because I had no clear distinction between the forms of unbelief, nor did I understand genuine versus counterfeit responses to God. But most important, I didn't know what the first and central issue really was: "What position will I take in regard to Jesus Christ?"
— Dr. Don

For Christ died for sins once for all, the righteous for the unrighteous, to bring you to God.

1 Peter 3:18

...if you confess with your mouth, "Jesus is Lord," and believe in your heart that God raised him from the dead, you will be saved.

Romans 10:9

Yet to all who received him, to those who believed in his name, he gave the right to become children of God...

John 1:12

On the other hand, a "yes" response to Jesus would mean the following:

1. I agree that Christ's substitutionary death on the cross for my sins opened the way to God.

2. I confess that Jesus is lord and is resurrected from the dead.

3. As a result of my confession of faith God declares me to be his child.

But remember, your "yes" is an unconditional surrender to God, not a contract with added conditions.

COUNTERFEIT FAITH

I'm giving my life to God ("I'll go to church every Sunday") on the condition that he will bless and reward me (help me ace all my tests, provide money for a great car and get rid of this acne). I will make demands of God and be good in order to earn God's approval.

GENUINE FAITH

I surrender my life unconditionally to God with repentance for my sins. I am forgiven and accepted by his love and grace alone. I am motivated to do good because of my love for him, and am able to do so because the Holy Spirit lives in me.

God promises to forgive all sin and to prepare a wonderful place in heaven to all who trust. He does not promise that this life will be free from problems and pain, only that he will love us and strengthen us in all circumstances. The Bible is clear that as long as we live in this world, we will have an adversary—Satan (or the devil)—whose goal is to discourage us and tempt us not to trust God.[1]

Through a series of imaginary letters, C. S. Lewis writes about the devil's strategies in his book, *The Screwtape Letters*. The letters are from Screwtape (a professional devil and tempter) to Wormwood (a junior tempter). In one of his letters, Screwtape writes to Wormwood about the greatest threat to the devil in our lives:

> *Do not be deceived, Wormwood, our cause is never more in danger than when a human, no longer desiring, but still intending, to do our Enemy's [in this case God's] will, looks around upon a universe from which every trace of Him seems to have vanished, and asks why he has been forsaken, and still obeys.*[2]

C. S. Lewis makes this point to encourage us not to despair of life when God's presence seems gone and we feel abandoned. The devil knows that a faith that is not conditional to how we feel or to our circumstances will thwart his deceptive schemes. Screwtape's description even fits Jesus as he hung on the cross. He was not a victim, he chose to be there. And when circumstances turned dark ("My God, my God, why have you forsaken me?"), he modeled perfect trust and stayed there. That's unconditional genuine faith.

We believe in Jesus because we are persuaded that he is God, not because of what we can get from him.

THINK ABOUT IT

1. Explain the difference between genuine and counterfeit faith.

   _____

   _____

   _____

2. Why do you think that counterfeit faith often leads to bitterness and disappointment?_____

3. Can you think of examples of real people who have exhibited genuine faith in the midst of hard times?_____

   _____

What Difference
Does Faith Make?
unit five - day five

We believe in Jesus because we are persuaded that he is God, not because of what we can get from him. Yet his presence in our lives should make a difference. Indeed, Jesus himself promised some changes as a result of a faith relationship with him.

   1. Jesus said. "I have come that they may have life, and have it to the full."[1]
   When we are in a faith relationship with God through Jesus, we become more not less, and move closer and closer to becoming all that God intended us to be.

After all, if we want to know how a product can best be used, we read the manufacturer's instructions. Likewise, since God is our creator, his guidelines for our life should maximize our fulfillment intellectually, morally and emotionally.

   2. Jesus said, "Let not your heart be troubled; believe...in me. In my Father's house are many dwelling places...I go to prepare a place for you. ...I will come again, and receive you to myself; that where I am, there you may be also."[2] We are in a genuine faith relationship with God, we have assurance of life after death.

Where do you want to be?

Are you willing to affirm that Jesus is alive, wants to give you new life and is coming to earth again in the future to take you to live with him forever?

Perhaps you're hesitating based on fear of what others might think. If so, remember that the Bible warns there will always be scoffers of God's promises. People scoffed at the time of Noah, too. But when the flood came, Noah looked like a genius and was saved because he had believed God and trusted his Word.

The Bible tells us that Jesus has delayed his promised return for a reason: He wants everyone to have the opportunity to choose life.

> First of all, you must understand that in the last days scoffers will come, scoffing and following their own evil desires. They will say, "Where is this 'coming' He promised?"
>
> **2 Peter 3-4**

WHY IS JESUS SLOW TO KEEP HIS PROMISE?

The apostle Peter says, "He is patient with you, not wanting anyone to perish, but everyone to come to repentance."

2 Peter 3:9

I remember coming to the point in my life when I realized that I no longer had any intellectual reasons against faith in Christ. But to my surprise, I was cautious, holding back and not eager to take that faith step. What was keeping me from letting go and allowing Jesus Christ to be in control of my life? Later I realized what it was—something very powerful. Only God was adequate to overcome the single most important factor that had kept me from faith in Jesus Christ. And when he did, my faith search came to a wonderful conclusion. I'll explain that next.

– Dr. Don

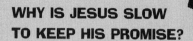

THINK ABOUT IT

1. Describe any fears or excuses you have (or had in the past) about turning your life over to God.

_____

_____

_____

2. According the Bible, what difference does Jesus' presence make in a person's life?

_____

_____

_____

unit six

Finding Real Life in Jesus

Seek and You Shall Find— and Be Found

unit six - day one

A college student who had attended one of my classes once called unexpectedly from his home during the summer break. After a friendly greeting, he talked in detail about an opportunity that was open to him. He was also very flattering to me as he went on and on. Finally, I interjected, "Why did you call?" I was ready for him to get to the "bottom line." He then admitted that he needed $1,500.

The "bottom line" principle

There is also a spiritual "bottom line." In my own search for God, I spent many months discovering the evidence for the Christian faith. I also discussed it with several people and weighed the pros and cons of affirming Jesus Christ through faith. But the time came when I had to ask the question, "What is the spiritual bottom line?" What would I do with what I knew was true? Only then did I realize that deep inside me was a difficult spiritual factor that was keeping me from faith in Jesus. I call it the "bottom line" principle.

This principle is illustrated by an incident that happened to the fisherman, Peter, before he became a believer and apostle of Jesus.[1] After fishing all night without catching anything, Peter and his crew were on shore cleaning their nets—and probably not in a very good mood.

Jesus, a carpenter and religious teacher—and novice fisherman— suggested they go out and drop the nets once more. At this point, Peter showed respect for Jesus by calling him "master" (or teacher), but did not recognize his deity. Peter was clearly reluctant, as his crew had most likely already tried every technique they knew that day. He was confident of the result—they wouldn't catch any fish, and they would just have to reclean the nets. As the "pro," he reminded his crew that this was Jesus' idea, not his. He thought he knew better than the traveling rabbi.

> Simon [Peter] answered, "Master, we've worked hard all night and haven't caught anything. But because you say so, I will let down the nets."
>
> **Luke 5:5**

FOR MEMORY

Ask and it will be given to you; seek and you will find; knock and the door will be opened to you. For everyone who asks receives; he who seeks finds; and to him who knocks, the door will be opened.

Matthew 7:7-8

GREEK MEANING

After the big catch, when Peter called Jesus "Lord," he used the Greek word "kurios." Sometimes this simply means "sir," but in many cases it was a reference to "Jehovah," the name of God. Peter's reaction suggests he meant it as a reference to Jesus as God.

But Peter didn't stay smug for long. As soon as the fishermen let down their nets again, they caught so many fish the nets began to break. Peter's response was very significant. Kneeling at Jesus' feet, he identified himself as a "sinful man." He then referred to Jesus as "Lord." Peter's sudden humility and act of worship after the catch indicate that he then recognized the deity of Jesus.

The following diagram helps us to visualize the spiritual "bottom line" principle. It illustrates the change in Peter's perception of himself and his understanding of Jesus.

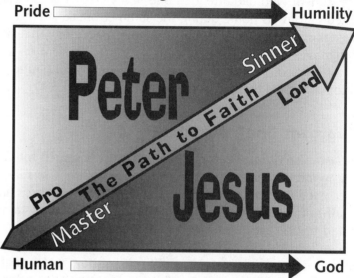

Think of the upper triangle (within the rectangle) as representing Peter and the lower one as representing Jesus. Before the miraculous catch of fish, Peter thinks he is the "pro" (illustrated by the base of his triangle on the left). Jesus? He's just the teacher and not very important (illustrated by the point of Jesus' triangle on the left). The diagonal from left to right represents the unfolding of the story and also the path to faith. As both boats become filled with fish, the upper triangle representing Peter becomes smaller, and the lower triangle representing Jesus becomes larger. On the right side of the rectangle, Jesus is now "Lord" and Peter has become a humble sinner in comparison.

The pride issue

Peter's fishing encounter with Jesus revealed his pride and self-sufficiency. It could have prevented him from a commitment to follow Jesus. Indeed, pride is very often the issue that prevents people from embracing Jesus Christ as Savior from their sin and Lord of their life. It is the spiritual "bottom line."

We may be intellectually persuaded that Jesus is Lord and God. We may even claim to be Christians and act like we think a Christian should. But self-sufficiency and pride may keep us from acknowledging that we need him. As long as we are so proud that we think we can "handle it," we won't see the need for Jesus in our lives—and we won't kneel at his feet and allow him to direct our lives.

Pride is often the spiritual "bottom line."

Jesus said to the self-righteous and proud Pharisees, "It is not the healthy who need a doctor, but the sick. I have not come to call the righteous, but sinners to repentance.

Mark 2:17

THINK ABOUT IT

The cocky kind of self-righteous pride that makes us feel that we know more or are better than others differs from the kind of pride referred to when someone says, "You can feel proud of the job you did." Try to think of times in your life when you can identify both kinds of pride. How did each impact your attitude about yourself?

_____

_____

_____

_____

Learning Humility

unit six - day two

John the Baptist and Moses are two people whom God used in big ways. The spiritual "bottom line" principle is illustrated in their lives as well as in the lives of many other biblical people.

John the Baptist was six months older than Jesus. Living a life of personal denial, his entire focus was to announce the coming of Jesus the Messiah. John had many disciples, was quite popular and had made great sacrifices for his successful ministry.

When Jesus began his own ministry, he soon attracted even more followers than John. Apparently, John's followers became jealous, thinking Jesus was infringing on John's territory. But when they complained, John refused to share their jealousy. Instead he responded humbly, saying, "After me comes a man who has a higher rank than I—the thong of whose sandal I am not worthy to untie." He added, "A man can receive nothing unless it has been given him from heaven...He must increase, but I must decrease."[1]

No wonder Jesus later highly praised John saying, "I tell you, among those born of women there is no one greater than John." How many famous people today would humbly allow someone else to take their limelight? John did so because his faith taught him the humility to accept God's eternal will rather than temporal fame. He understood and applied the spiritual bottom line principle.

Moses is one of the most well-known biblical figures. Like John the Baptist, the key to Moses' greatness late in life was his discovery of the "bottom line" spiritual principle. Moses learned it the hard way.

He was born to slave parents in Egypt at a time when the Pharaoh had declared a death sentence on male Hebrew newborns. Desperate to save his life, Moses' mother put him in a basket among the reeds near the bank of the Nile River behind the royal palace. Pharaoh's daughter found him and raised him as her own son. As a result, Moses grew up enjoying all the luxury and privileges of royalty.

> John the Baptist described Jesus as "the Lamb of God who takes away the sin of the world."
>
> John 1:29

> "A man can receive nothing unless it has been given him from heaven. ...He must increase, but I must decrease."
>
> John 3:27,30

When I was a competitive college student, I would have been angry with anyone who took from me the attention and glory I received for my athletic and academic achievements. I know that I did not have the humility of John the Baptist.

– Dr. Don

A LATE BLOOMER

Moses is considered a hero by Jews and Christians alike. However, few people realize that his spiritual reputation is based entirely on his life after the age of 80.

Moses was the "big man" in the palace—the "pro!" His pride led him to think that he could use his power and any means to save the Hebrews from their slavery.

MOSES' HIDEAWAY
The desert where Moses fled and spent 40 years is modern Saudi Arabia.

"Who am I?" or better, "Who do I think I am?" This was the bottom line question that I faced in my own spiritual life. More than anything else, my reluctance to admit my own moral failure and need kept me from confessing faith in Jesus as my Lord.
– Dr. Don

At age 40, Moses was the most educated and powerful Jew of his day. Because of that, he began to intervene in Hebrew disputes, acting as an arbitrator or judge. Then he committed treason by killing an Egyptian guard who was beating a Hebrew slave. What motivated his actions? The Bible says that "...he supposed that his brethren understood that God was granting them deliverance through him."[2]

The key words in that verse are "he supposed." God didn't ask Moses to be the deliverer of the Hebrew people until 40 years later. Moses had likely acted out of his own sense of importance. Perhaps he thought that he was above the law. But his own people rebuffed him, and the Egyptians were about to put him to death for murder, so he fled into the desert. He spent the next 40 years as a nomad and shepherd, a loner in the desert. No vocational counselor would suggest a career of shepherding in the wilderness to the most educated and skilled Jew in the world. But this was God's prescription to rid Moses of a bad case of self-righteousness and pride. How many times must Moses have reflected on his failure, and how badly he had "blown it."

Moses asks God, "Who am I?"[3]

Then, after 40 years, God spoke to Moses from the midst of a burning bush: "Therefore, come now, and I will send you to Pharaoh, so that you may bring my people, the sons of Israel, out of Egypt."

If God had said that to him 40 years earlier, Moses may have thought, "God, I don't know you very well, but I have to hand it to you. You certainly know how to pick 'em. If anyone can do the job, I can."

A NEW MAN
At 40, Moses had been the most educated and skilled Jew in the world—the prideful "pro." At 80, he was a humbled man who recognized his need for God in order to truly succeed in life.

But after wandering as a shepherd for 40 years in the wilderness, Moses responded: "Who am I, that I should go to Pharaoh, and that I should bring the sons of Israel out of Egypt?" This humble response was the mark of a changed Moses. But he still needed to understand the full significance of his question, "Who am I?"

God told Moses, "Certainly I will be with you...." The implication is clear. When Moses had tried to save his people 40 years earlier, he had tried to do so on his own—and he failed. This time, it wouldn't depend on Moses' adequacy, but on the power of God working through him.

Moses asks God, "Who are you?"

Even though God spoke directly to him, Moses was cautious about going back to Egypt. Would his own people want anything to do with him? He still had painful memories of the rejection he felt when they sneered, "Who made you a ruler and judge over us?"[4] Fearing a repeat of this taunt, Moses asked, "God, who are you?" God's answer is awesome: "I Am who I Am." Moses was to go back to Egypt as the instrument of God who is without beginning or end, the eternal one.

Moses still questioned: "What if they will not believe me...?" In response, God turned Moses' shepherd's crook into a snake and back again, and made his hand leprous like snow, then healed it again. By doing this, God made it clear that he has all the power in the universe. He didn't need Moses' education and skills to get the job done. God was inviting Moses to be a human instrument through whom God would channel his power. Moses agreed to give God all the glory and returned to Egypt. And through him God performed so many signs and wonders that the Pharaoh was eventually forced to free the Hebrew slaves.

Applying the spiritual principle

"Who am I?" and "God, who are you?" Each one of us must answer these two timeless questions in our faith relationship with Jesus Christ. As Moses did in his later life, we must learn the paradox of humility and power. Even though he was eulogized at his death for the "signs and wonders" that the Lord did through him, Moses was described as more humble than any man who "was on the face of the earth."[5] It is unlikely that he learned this humility in the palace in Egypt. Maybe more of us need to learn shepherding in the wilderness.

The questions "Who am I?" and "God, who are you?" were not clear in my mind at the time I was struggling with my own faith search. But the concept was. I realize that who I thought I was determined to a great extent how big my God could be. Yet, I was both hesitant and incapable of making myself smaller, so to speak. It wasn't until God personally revealed to me how big he was that I finally saw myself small in comparison. When that happened, the course of my life changed.

– Dr. Don

"In God you come up against something which is in every respect immeasurably superior to yourself. Unless you know God as that—and therefore, know yourself as nothing in comparison—you do not know God at all. As long as you are proud you cannot know God."

– C. S. Lewis

BIBLE DISCOVERY

Look up these Bible verses and fill in the blanks:
Proverbs 16:18-19; Proverbs 18:12; Matthew 23:12; 1 Peter 5:5-6

1. Identify the spiritual principle described in all these verses. How does this principle relate to Moses' life?_____

2. What is one of Jesus' qualities relevant to this chapter that he said we should learn from him? Matthew 11:29_____

3. Is boastful pride from God? If not, where? 1 John 2:16_____

4. Why do you think humbleness was one of the three most important qualities that God says are good and he expects in our lives? Micah 6:8

_____

My Faith Search

unit six - day three

My high school days

I grew up in a small, rural midwestern community. Of the many attributes I inherited from my parents, two have shaped most of my life. The first was my athletic ability. Conference, regional and state championships in various sports, especially baseball, gave me a basis for a big ego. The more ink I got in the newspaper for my athletic "performance," the more my ego grew. The coaches first noticed a problem when they had to issue me a larger football helmet for each week's game!

The second asset was intellectual ability. Good grades came easily for me, and my peers viewed me as a "brain." The recognition and awards that I got in the academic area further fueled a healthy dose of conceit and self-sufficiency. Although I attended a Christian church with my family, God seemed so distant. However, during a sophomore biology lab, I met a girl who was quite attractive to me. She was very capable but humble, giving credit for her achievements to God. She talked about Jesus as if she knew him personally. Vernee and I began to spend time together. Her influence set me on a spiritual search that lasted several years.

On to college

Being recruited by colleges and receiving a number of scholarship offers made me feel that I was in the driver's seat of my life. My college years saw more athletic exploits, academic achievements and social recognition (such as king of the campus Valentine ball).

> I was determined to help high school students avoid religious narrow-mindedness and turn to a more enlightened scientific understanding of life.

Intellectually, I was especially impressed with the logical and rational yet personable science professors who focused on scientific "facts"—not on subjective things like faith in God. I wanted to be like them, so I majored in biology and secondary education.

The height of my vanity as "the pro" came during my first year as a high school biology teacher. I had applied for future graduate study at a nearby university. Shortly after Christmas that year, the head of the biology department called to congratulate me on my

Each person's faith search is different because we are uniquely created and have different life experiences. Yet, those who have found faith also find many things in common. Testimonies provide opportunities for us to learn from and offer hope to one another.

Some of you will identify more closely with my story than others. As you read it, consider the following questions:

How have your natural abilities, your successes or failures impacted the way you think about yourself—and about God?

When did you first recognize your need for God?

What has most motivated you in your faith search?
– Dr. Don

I met some Christians who didn't fit my earlier impression that Christians were anti-intellectual. Some of them were even university scientists. They weren't pushy about their faith, but when I challenged it, they defended it with evidences that I never knew existed. Over and over my research led me to focus on the person of Jesus. I liked his manner—compassionate, witty, sensitive, powerful and moral. But some of his teachings were threatening to me.
—Dr. Don

He mocks proud mockers, but gives grace to the humble.

Proverbs 3:34

acceptance to graduate school and to announce that I'd received a national scholarship that would pay all living and educational expenses for the next four years while I pursued a Ph.D. degree.

Such wonderful news should have brought tears of gratefulness, but I'm ashamed to recall my thoughts as I hung up the phone: "When you're good enough, this kind of thing happens to you!" I felt I had earned that award because I was "good." I was on the ultimate ego trip—someday people would address me as doctor.

Discovering a lot I didn't know

However, soon after arriving at the university for graduate studies, I met some Christians who didn't fit my earlier impression that Christians were anti-intellectual. Some of them were even university scientists. They weren't pushy about their faith, but when I challenged it, they defended it with evidences that I never knew existed. A reasonable faith was appealing, but I wondered whether it was really true. Being competitive, I took up the challenge to find out. I read books on archaeology and ancient manuscripts. What a surprise to me that the New Testament writings were the most reliable ancient works known. Although I had learned about the Bible as a child, I had never examined its truthfulness.

> Hello...!
> God must have had a good laugh, so to speak, over my thinking that I had the world by the tail.

As I applied the tools of evidence and reason to investigating Christian faith, little by little it dawned on me that my skepticism had been based on false information. Over and over my research led me to focus on the person of Jesus. I liked his manner—compassionate, witty, sensitive, powerful and moral. But some of his teachings were threatening to me—absolute authority of God, uncompromising holiness and unlimited forgiveness, even toward enemies. Like Peter, the fishing "pro," I thought that—in these matters—I just knew better than Jesus did.

The big turning point

By the way, remember the girl in high school biology? Vernee and I got married in college. It was after our marriage and in the midst of my finishing up graduate school that my life took a dramatic turn.

One night, my wife Vernee had gone to bed leaving me alone to hit the books into the wee hours of the morning. For some reason, I picked up the Bible instead and was drawn to the Old Testament book of Job. If you haven't read the story, it's about a very wealthy man with a great family, tons of friends and faith in God.[1]

One day the devil told God that he was sure Job would curse God if he didn't have it so good. He asked permission to bring some suffering into Job's life to prove that Job would buckle.[2] Things went from bad to worse for Job. He lost his possessions and his children, and was inflicted with boils all over his body.

I read through the book with great interest. As disaster upon disaster came to Job, I judged God as unfair. I agreed with Job when he cried out, "God has wronged me."[3]

Job then asked to have a hearing before God to question God.[4] Job got his chance. But it was God who asked all the questions.[5]

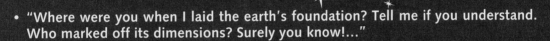

- "Where were you when I laid the earth's foundation? Tell me if you understand. Who marked off its dimensions? Surely you know!..."

- "Have you ever given orders to the morning, or shown the dawn its place..."

- "Can you bind the beautiful Pleiades? Can you loose the cords of Orion? Can you bring forth the constellations in the seasons..."

- "Who endowed the heart with wisdom or gave understanding to the mind?..."

Suddenly it occurred to me that God was into science, something I was good at. But these questions were deeper, identifying the design, the precision and the predictability of the laws of nature. And, as if placed there just for me, God turned to questions about biology:

- "Do you know when the mountain goats give birth? Do you watch when the doe bears her fawn?"

- "Does the hawk take flight by your wisdom and spread his wings toward the south? Does the eagle soar at your command and build his nest on high?"

I sensed that the ability to pass a multiple-choice test on these questions was not the point. After many more questions about the creation, God gave Job a chance to respond: "Will the one who contends with the Almighty correct him? Let him who accuses God answer him!"[6]

Job's response was not what I expected. "I am unworthy—how can I reply to you? I put my hand over my mouth...I have no answer." In my conceit, I thought Job had wimped out. What kind of answer was that to such profound questions? Surely he could do better than that! Of course, I was not in the presence of God as Job was.[7]

God continued, "Would you discredit my justice? Would you condemn me to justify yourself? Do you have an arm like God's and can your voice thunder like his?" Unleash the fury of your wrath, look at every proud man and bring him low.... Then I myself will admit to you that your own right hand can save you!"[8]

Breakthrough in my faith search

Two more chapters of questions about the design in nature followed.[9] Suddenly, in a very personal way, God was no longer talking to Job —he was talking to me! Powerfully (though I heard no voice), I experienced God questioning me: "Don, who do you think you are anyway?" My mind's eye flashed back to the many times I was filled with arrogance and pride. I was convicted of my self-sufficiency, independence and conceit. In contrast, I was now seeing the power, wisdom and glory of the infinite God. Job's final remarks describe what was going through my mind:

"I know that you can do all things; no plan of yours can be stopped. My ears heard of you but now my eyes have seen you. Therefore I despise myself and repent in dust and ashes."[10]

I went to my knees beside my chair and began to cry. Although I held the stereotype that big people don't cry—I thought it was a sign of weakness in a man—that night it didn't matter. I was overwhelmed by my sinfulness and said over and over, "I'm sorry. Lord, I'm sorry."

As I was still reflecting on the awesomeness of God, the unexpected happened. The realization came to me that I was free— free of my need to win, to be number one and to prove myself— free of the slavery to my ego. What a release not to have to perform to be accepted! God's love through the sacrifice of Jesus on the cross, the Lamb of God, had met the just demands of the Law. If I turned in trust to Jesus, God promised forgiveness and salvation as his gift to me. My tears became tears of joy and my heart cried, "Thank you. Lord, thank you. Thank you!" I was a new man, forgiven and free.

Life changes—for here and forever

Many years have passed since I first acknowledged my need of a Savior. In a real sense, Jesus found me. I went on to earn my Ph.D. in biology and later went to seminary where I earned an M.A. in New Testament studies. But I was no longer motivated by my ego. I was now accountable to Jesus who was my creator and will be my ultimate judge. His love and discipline motivate me to serve and to become all that God created me to be.

Powerfully (though I heard no voice), I experienced God questioning me: "Don, who do you think you are anyway?"
–Dr. Don

What Jesus has done in my life

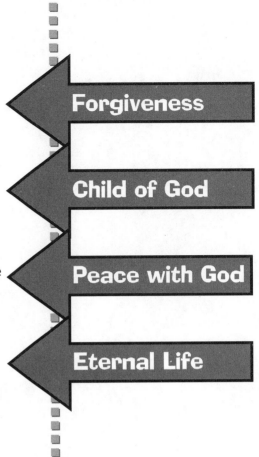

1. **I have received and continue to experience the forgiveness of my sin.** The Bible says, "If we confess our sins, he is faithful and just and will forgive us our sins and purify us from all unrighteousness." 1 John 1:9

2. **I am a spiritual child of God and am enabled to follow him by the Holy Spirit within me.** The Bible says: "Yet to all who received him, to those who believed in his name, he gave the right to become children of God." John 1:12

3. **I am at peace with God, and do not fear judgment.** The Bible says: "For God did not send the Son into the world to judge the world, but that the world should be saved through Him. He who believes in Him is not judged. . ." John 3:17,18a

4. **I have the assurance of eternal life after death.** Jesus said: "I am the resurrection and the life; he who believes in Me shall live even if he dies. . ." John 11:25

My wife, Vernee, and I both recognize that we would not have stayed together in our marriage these many years if not for the grace to forgive and change—which comes from God. In addition, since our two sons have both affirmed Jesus as their Savior, there is the assurance that when our relationship here must end, death will only serve to reunite us once again, this time for eternity. Every aspect of my life has been enriched as a result of knowing Jesus.

How to Experience
Real Life in Jesus
unit six - day four

Knowing and experiencing real life in Jesus requires an understanding and acceptance of four basic truths found in the Bible.

1. Sin is a universal condition of all people.
It results in separation from God and death.

"...sin entered into the world, and death through sin, and so death spread to all men, because all sinned..."

Romans 5:12

"...for there is no distinction, for all have sinned..."
Romans 3:22b-23

"But your Iniquities [sins] have separated you from your God."

Isaiah 59:2
Also see John 8:24

2. Jesus Christ has provided the only way back to God.
His death was a substitute to redeem us from sin into a forgiven relationship with God, and his resurrection removed death's power over us.

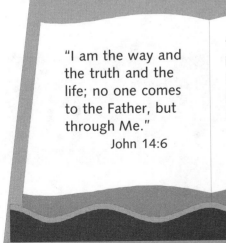

"I am the way and the truth and the life; no one comes to the Father, but through Me."
John 14:6

"And there is salvation in no one else; for there is no other name under heaven...by which we must be saved."
Acts 4:12
Also see John 1:29;
Matthew 1:21

3. God's forgiveness through Jesus Christ's death must be affirmed by a personal response.

"Repent, then, and turn to God, so that your sins may be wiped out...."
Acts 3:19 Also see I John 1:9

"... if you confess with your mouth, Jesus is Lord, and believe in your heart that God raised Him from the dead, you will be saved."   *Romans 10:9*
Also see Acts 2:37-38; Acts 16:30-34

4. God's act of grace in those who personally affirm faith in Jesus Christ includes the creation of new life within by the Holy Spirit who comes to live in them, and the gift and assurance of eternal life.

"Yet to all who received Him, to those who believed in His name, He gave the right to become children of God—children born not of natural descent ... but born of God."   John 1:12

"Don't you know that you yourselves are God's temple and that God's Spirit lives in you?"   I Corinthians 3:16

"...the free gift of God is eternal life in Christ Jesus our Lord."
                              Romans 6:23b

"These things I have written to you who believe in the name of the Son of God, in order that you may know that you have eternal life."
                              I John 5:13

BIBLE DISCOVERY

John's gospel records more than 20 people who met and found real life in Jesus.

Read John 1:35-41. Who discovered real life in Jesus here?_____

What did he call Jesus?_____

Read John 4:7-42. Who discovered real life in Jesus here?_____

Because of her, the Samaritans discovered Jesus, too. What did they call Jesus?

(v.42)_____

Read John 9:1-41. Who discovered real life in Jesus here?_____

What did he initially think of Jesus? (v.17)_____

How did he eventually respond to Jesus? (v.38)_____

Read John 20:19-29. Who discovered real life in Jesus here?_____

What did he call Jesus?_____

Now turn to the next chapter to personally discover new life in Jesus for yourself.

An Invitation
to Find Real Life in Jesus
unit six - day five

Jesus would speak to the crowds that gathered around him and say, "Come and follow me." On another occasion he said it this way: "Come to me, all you who are weary and burdened, and I will give you rest. Take my yoke upon you and learn from me, for I am gentle and humble in heart, and you will find rest for your souls. For my yoke is easy and my burden is light."

Jesus and his promises will not be real for you unless you reach out and embrace them for yourself. The four biblical truths about how to know and experience God have been summarized in the prayer below. Your faith search has led you to Jesus. Tell him through prayer that you want real life. Use the prayer below as a guide.

A SIMPLE PRAYER TO FIND REAL LIFE

Dear God,

I want to know you as a reality in my life. I acknowledge that my sin has resulted in separation from you. I repent and affirm Jesus Christ as my Lord and risen Savior because he gave his life on the cross as my substitute to redeem me. Thank you for the gift of forgiveness, salvation, and the Holy Spirit within who will direct my life and enable me to understand and follow your Word from this day on. Thank you, too, for making me your spiritual child and giving me the assurance of eternal life when I die. I love you. Amen.

I would like to hear from you! If this book has helped you discover a new—or renewed—relationship with Jesus Christ, I encourage you to write or call my office about it. My staff would be happy to talk with you, and to send you a gift—a free Bible study to help you make the most of this new relationship with Christ. (You'll find my address at the bottom of this page.)

Of course, the Bible study I'll send you is only a start, so talk with your pastor or youth leader about how to keep growing in your faith. Believe me, following Jesus Christ is the greatest adventure anywhere. So make the most of it!

My prayers are with you.
— Dr. Don

ANOTHER STEP

If this has been your sincere prayer, let me be the first to welcome you into the family of God. Please do two things right now:

1. **Turn back in your** *FaithSearch* **book to page 121, and read/ reflect on the four things that Jesus has done in your life. The "I" is now "YOU!"**

2. **Call, write or e-mail me to request a free Bible study.**

Jesus promised, *"...I came that they might have life, and might have it abundantly." (John 10:10)* I would be happy to help you to experience life to the full as he said. If you have affirmed Jesus Christ as your Savior and Lord as a result of this *FaithSearch* study, please call or write and share that with me. I will send a free Bible study that has been designed to encourage your spiritual growth. A growing life of faith will enable you to trust God with every detail of your life.

The Bible says, *"And now just as you trusted Christ to save you, trust him, too, for each day's problems...See that you go on growing in the Lord, and become strong and vigorous in the truth you were taught."* **Colossians 2:6-7 (LB)**

I pray that real life in Jesus will fill you through and through. I look forward to hearing from you.

Call, write or e-mail for your free Bible study.

Dr. Don Bierle
Faith Studies International
P.O. Box 786
Chanhassen, MN 55317
Phone: (952) 401-4501 or 1-800-964-1447
FAX: (952) 401-4504
e-mail address: FSMN@FaithStudies.org
www.faithstudies.org

FaithSearch

NOTES

Unit One, Day Four
1. Paul Little, *Know Why You Believe* (Downers Grove: InterVarsity, 1988), p. 15.

Unit Two, Day Two
1. Norman L. Geisler, and William E. Nix, *A General Introduction to the Bible* (Chicago: Moody, 1968), pp. 385f.
2. Josh McDowell, *Evidence that Demands a Verdict* (San Bernardino: Here's Life, 1979), p. 46.
3. Bruce M. Metzger, *Chapters in the History of New Testament Textual Criticism* (Grand Rapids: Eerdmans, 1963), cited in Geisler and Nix, *A General Introduction to the Bible* (Chicago: Moody, 1968), pp. 366f.
4. Carsten Thiede and Matthew D'Ancona, *Eyewitnesses to Jesus* (New York: Doubleday, 1966).

Unit Two, Day Three
1. Flavius Josephus, *Antiquities of the Jews* (Grand Rapids: AP&A), book XVIII, ch.3, paragraph 3, p. 379.
2. F. F. Bruce, *Jesus and Christian Origins outside the New Testament* (Grand Rapids: Eerdmans, 1974), p. 22.
3. Luke 2:1; Luke 3:1-2
4. Luke 3:1-2
5. Zvi Greenhut, "Burial Cave of the Caraphas Family" and Ronny Reich, "Caiaphas Name Inscribed on Bone Boxes," *Biblical Archaeology Review* 18 (Sept/Oct 1992): 28-44.
6. Robert Bull, "Caesarea Maritima—The Search for Herod's City," *Biblical Archaeology Review* 8 (May/June 1982): 24-41.
7. Acts 17:6
8. *The New International Dictionary of Biblical Archaeology* (Grand Rapids: Zondervan, 1983), Blaiklock and Harrison, editors, p. 367.
9. Josh McDowell, *Evidence that Demands a Verdict* (San Bernardino: Here's Life, 1972), p.75.
10. William Ramsay, *The Bearing of Recent Discovery on the Trustworthiness of the New Testament* (Grand Rapids: Baker reprint, 1979), p. 222.

Unit Two Day Four
1. Genesis 19:24
2. Clifford Wilson, *Ebla Tablets: Secrets of a Forgotten City* (San Diego: Master Books, 1979), pp. 36-37.
3. Aharon Kempinski, "Hittites in the Bible—What Does Archeology Say?" *Biblical Archaeology Review* 5 (Sept/Oct. 1979): 20-44.
4. Luke 2:1-5
5. William Ramsay, *The Bearing of Recent Discovery on the Trustworthiness of the New Testament* (Grand Rapids: Baker, 1979), pp. 238ff.
6. A. N. Sherwin White, *Roman Society and Law in the New Testament*, (Oxford: Clarendon, 1963), cited in Clark Pinnock, *A Case for Faith*, (Minneapolis: Bethany Fellowship, 1980). p. 77
7. Vassilios Tzaferis, "Crucifixion—The Archaeological Evidence," *Biblical Archaeology Review* 9. (Jan/Feb 1985): 44-53.
8. John 19:31-33
9. Millar Burrows, *What Mean These Stones?* (New York: Meridian Books, 1956), p. 1.
10. Kenyon, *The Bible and Archaeology* (New York: Harper and Row, 1940), p. 279.
11. K. A. Kitchen, *The Bible in its World* (Downers Grove: InterVarsity, 1977), p. 132.

Unit Two, Day Five
1. Acts 2:1, 22-24
2. Acts 2:4-1

Unit Three, Day One
1. Luke 4:16-23; Luke 4:22-23
2. Isaiah 9:6
3. Matthew 22:41-46
4. John 8:53-58

Unit Three, Day One (Cont.)

5. Exodus 3:14
6. John 10:30-33.
7. John 11: 25-26
8. John 19:7

Unit Three, Day Two

1. John 9:2

Unit Three - day Three

1. Luke 7:11-16
2. John 10:37-38

Unit Three, Day Four

1. Luke 9:20
2. George H. Gallup, Jr., *Religion in America* (Princeton Religion Research Center, 1996), p. 16.
3. Jon Buell and O. Quentin Hyder, *Jesus: God, Ghost or Guru?* (Grand Rapids, Zondervan, 1978), p. 102
4. Gary R. Habermas, *Ancient Evidence for the Life of Jesus* (Nashville: Thomas Nelson, 1984), pp. 87ff.
5. Acts 9:1-18; Acts 22,26
6. Lee Strobel, *The Case for Christ* (Grand Rapids: Zondervan, 1998), p. 266

Unit Three, Day Five

1. John 2:19
2. Luke 24:11
3. Paul Maier, *First Easter* (San Francisco: Harper and Row, 1982), p. 120.
4. 1 Corinthians 15:6
5. John 7:3-5
6. Acts 15:13; 21; 18
7. Acts 22 & 26
8. Mark 14:50, 66-72.
9. Josh McDowell, *Evidence that Demands a Verdict* (San Bernardino: Here's Life, 1972), p.201.
10. C. S. Lewis, *Mere Christianity* (New York: Macmillan, 1952), pp. 55-56
11. John 11:25-26

Unit Four, Day One

1. Romans 10:17 (Phillips)

Unit Four, Day Three

1. Genesis 22:17-18
2. See Genesis 22 for this section on Abraham and Isaac
3. Hebrews 11:17-19

Unit Four, Day Four

1. John 7:37-39
2. Quoted in Josh McDowell, *Evidence that Demands a Verdict* (San Bernardino: Here's Life, 1979), p. 361.
3. Ephesians 1:13-14
4. John 3:3-8
5. Josh McDowell, *Evidence that Demands a Verdict* (San Bernardino: Here's Life, 1979), p. 361.
6. Luke 9:20

Unit Four, Day Five

1. 1 Timothy 1:13

Unit Five, Day One

1. Elizabeth Elliott, *Through Gates of Splendor*, (New York: Harper and Brothers, 1957).

Unit Five, Day Two

1. Numbers 11:4-6
2. Numbers 14:6-9
3. Numbers 14:30-34

Unit Five, Day Three

1. Luke 7:6-7
2. Genesis 6:8-9
3. Genesis 6:22

Unit Five, Day Four

1. John 8:44; 1 Peter 5:8
2. C. S. Lewis, *The Screwtape Letters* (Chicago: Lord and King Associates, 1976), p. 51.

Unit Five, Day Five

1. John 10:10
2. John 14:1-3

Unit Six, Day One

1. Luke 5:1-8

Unit Six, Day Two

1. John 3:30
2. Acts 7:25
3. Acts 7:27
4. See Exodus 3 for this section
5. See Deuteronomy 34:10-12 and Numbers 12:3 for this paradox.

Unit Six, Day Three

1. Job 1:1-3
2. Job 1:7-12
3. Job 19:6-3
4. Job 13:15,18
5. Job 38:1-39:30
6. Job 40:1-2
7. Job 40:3-5
8. Job 40:8-14
9. Job 40 and 41
10. Job 42:1-6

Resources to help you grow and share your faith

FaithQuest multimedia CD-ROM

A fully interactive presentation of evidences for Christian faith that features:
- Complete text of *Surprised by Faith*
- Hot-buttons to access photos, charts, video and audio footage.
- 65 minutes of Faith Study video.

Use *FaithQuest* to share your faith with a computer enthusiast! Available for IBM-compatible PCs only. Minimum system requirements: 486-33 / 8 MB RAM / Windows 3.1 or Windows 95.
Price: $19 plus postage & handling.

The Owner's Manual

An ideal tool for building your relationship with Jesus. This workbook contains eight easy-to-follow lessons that help a new Christian get firmly rooted in the truth. Each lesson leads you through key Scripture passages that help you understand what God has done and will do in your life. Ideal for individual follow-up and discipleship of people carrying spiritual "baggage" from broken relationships, abuse, and other issues. (80 pages, 8-1/2 x 11 paperback.)
Price: $6 plus postage & handling.

The Faith Study VIDEO

In six stimulating sessions—divided into 11 parts of approximately 30 minutes each—Dr. Don Bierle offers sound reasons for a living faith. This presentation, that has challenged and changed the lives of thousands of people, is useful as a youth or adult education elective, as an evangelistic study, or as a means of private study. The video was professionally produced before a live audience. (6 VHS tapes in attractive albums, 300 minutes.)

A free *Leader's Guide* ($10 retail value) is included, enabling you to expand the Faith Study to an 11-week quarterly elective, or guiding you through the steps to conduct a successful 6-session outreach home series.

Also free with your set of six Faith Study video tapes:
- *Seminar Student Manual* (52 pp., 8-1/2 x 11)—retail value $4.00.
- *Surprised by Faith* (128 pp., trade paperback)—retail value $8.99.
- *The Owner's Manual* (80 pp., 8-1/2 x 11)—retail value $6.00

Price: $99 plus postage & handling.

The Faith Study AUDIO

The same presentation as the Faith Study video series, the Faith Study audio is an ideal format for the commuter or exerciser. Do you have a co-worker or neighbor with whom you'd like to share the gospel? Lend these tapes to that person and be prepared for some amazing responses! (6 audio cassettes in an attractive album, 300 minutes.)
Price: $30 plus $3 postage & handling—add $1.00 postage for each additional set.

Surprised by Faith BOOK

Dr. Don Bierle shares his personal discovery of faith in this very readable book. A former skeptic, the author recounts the evidence and reasons that satisfied his questioning mind. A convenient, effective way to share the evidence for faith, this attractive book expands on the Faith Study and complements it by providing documentation and discussion questions. (Many people buy several copies and lend them out or give them as gifts.) Contains many illustrations and charts. (128 pages, quality paperback). Publisher's retail price: $8.99. *Price: $7 plus postage & handling.*

To order any of the above items, call or write:

Faith Studies International
P. O. Box 786
Chanhassen, MN 55317
Phone: (952) 401-4501
Toll-free 1-800-964-1447
Fax: (952) 401-4504
VISA and MasterCard accepted

Study Notes

Study Notes

Study Notes

Study Notes

Study Notes

Study Notes

Study Notes

Study Notes

Study Notes

Study Notes

Study Notes